Gaia Warriors

First U.S. edition 2011

Library of Congress Cataloging-in-Publication Data is available.

Library of Congress Catalog Card Number pending

ISBN 978-0-7636-4808-4

10 11 12 13 14 15 16 CCP 10 9 8 7 6 5 4 3 2 1

Printed in Shenzhen, Guangdong, China

This book was typeset in American Typewriter, AT Arta, and ITC Bookman.

The interior of this book was printed on 100% recycled paper.

Candlewick Press
99 Dover Street
Somerville, Massachusetts 02144

visit us at www.candlewick.com

GAIA WARRIORS

URGENT

THE FIGHT IS ON!

Nicola Davies

with an afterword by
James Lovelock

CANDLEWICK PRESS

CONTENTS

Section Two
Gaia Warriors

Section Three
Afterword by James Lovelock

Abel & Col*

*Please look after our box, keep it dry, and leave it out for us.
You never know... you might see it again someday.

bikeit

B I K E

INTRODUCTION

Most people don't like change. They see it as scary or uncomfortable or both. But if nothing ever changed, we'd still be sitting in caves chewing on old mammoth bones. Ever since the Big Bang, our universe has always changed. So we shouldn't be too scared by the fact that the climate of our home planet is changing now, and that we will have to change too, if we are to survive.

This book is about **how** and *why* the earth's climate is changing. But it is also about the **people,** all over the world, who are finding ways for humans to live without hurting our planet. As you read this book, you'll be hearing from them: young and old, men and women, scientists, lawyers, businesspeople, architects, designers, moms and dads, kids and campaigners—all sorts of people; people just like you.

We all have a choice. We can carry on as usual and fry. Or we can take the opportunity climate change offers us to make a better world for everyone.

In other words, we can CHOOSE to change for the better.

"We must be the change we want to see in the world."

MAHATMA GANDHI

(Gandhi was an Indian political and spiritual leader in the first half of the twentieth century. He lived his ideals of nonviolent protest and sustainable living, and had a big impact all around the world.)

Climate Change: The Basics

66 **I can't understand why the reaction . . . to extreme climate change is to turn the newspaper over and start reading an article about the latest bikini trend.** 99

CARRI SWANN

(In 2006, when she was fifteen, Carri was chosen by Britain's Department of Environment, Food and Rural Affairs to be a "Climate Champion" and spread the word about climate change.)

The low-lying Netherlands have always suffered from floods, but rising sea levels have made people interested in buying floating houses like these.

www.ecoboot.nl

Eagan, Bluepeace

Piles of concrete blocks protect Male, the capital of the Maldives, from storms and rising sea levels.

UNLESS you've been hiding under a rock for the past several years, you've heard about climate change: all those scary predictions about melting ice caps, killer storms, rising sea levels, and severe droughts. But maybe you've been telling yourself, "Oh, it won't REALLY happen," or "It won't happen for a hundred years."

Well, it's happening right now, **already,** all over the world.

The sea ice in the Arctic is getting smaller, and in 2002 an ice shelf in Antarctica almost the size of Rhode Island broke up and disappeared. The strength of storms, cyclones, and hurricanes is increasing, and since the 1970s the number of people whose homes get flooded every year has risen from 40 million to 150 million. Male, the capital city of the Maldives (a country composed entirely of tiny islands in the Indian Ocean), has had to build a wall eleven feet high to keep out the rising sea, and the people of Tuvalu—another nation of islands, in the South Pacific—are trying to negotiate settlement rights in New Zealand for when their whole country disappears under the waves. The people of the Netherlands are building floating houses to prepare for the flooding of their low-lying country, while in Western Australia farmers are struggling with declines in rainfall that threaten to put them out of business.

Those are just a few of the many thousands of examples of the effects climate change is already having on human lives around the world. In our lifetimes and those of our children and grandchildren, climate change is going to be the biggest challenge human beings have ever had to face.

Yes, it's a real drag that we should be alive at **just** the time when everything is starting to go wrong, and yes, it **is** scary, but sticking our fingers in our ears and saying, "La-di-da, it's not happening!" isn't going to help. Neither is going around being gloomy and telling everyone you meet, "We're doomed, all doomed."

Climate change is happening, but we're not doomed. We can't stop it, but we could slow it down and we could prepare for its effects. It's going to be a big job, and it'll mean changing almost everything about the way we live now—how we light and heat our homes, what transportation we use, how we design buildings, how we grow food, how we handle disasters and diseases, and even how people and countries decide, together, what's fair and what isn't.

It isn't going to be easy, but it isn't going to be boring, either. In fact, we might all be about to participate in the most exciting period in human history. Forget Xbox and Wii, orcs, Sauron, and Voldemort; this is the REAL battle, the battle to save ourselves and our planet from climate catastrophe.

The good news about this battle is that it isn't going to involve guns, blood, and killing; the weapons you'll need to help fight it are ideas, energy, and determination. The even better news is that there are already lots of people out there fighting and actually enjoying being part of such an exciting and challenging struggle. Who knows? If you join them, you might just help save the world.

"Humans never change unless we have to. And finally, we have to."

SEVERN CULLIS SUZUKI

(Severn is a young Canadian activist who has been sticking up for our planet since she spoke to the 1992 United Nations Earth Summit in Rio de Janeiro when she was twelve.)

There are about a trillion books and websites that will tell you all you could ever possibly want to know about climate change (you'll find some of the most useful ones listed at the back of this book). The aim of Section One isn't to compete with all of those, but to give you a guide to some of the basic facts about what is happening to the earth and its climate. It's written in the form of answers to questions that people often ask about climate change, especially people who aren't sure that they really believe "the whole global warming thing." So even if you already know all there is to know, you might find the answers in this section useful if you're trying to convince someone that climate change isn't a worldwide conspiracy made up by job-seeking scientists and that the greenhouse effect is not a mental illness suffered by gardeners.

"Global warming — the great big lie. How can they say the Earth is warming up? Just look at our summers — once again this year it is rain, rain, rain, and more rain."

Contributor to a newspaper's online discussion

(Someone taking a short-sighted view of climate change and getting all mixed up.)

What Is Climate Change?

The first thing to understand is that **climate and weather are not the same thing.** As science-fiction writer Robert A. Heinlein once said, "Climate is what you expect, but weather is what you get." But you already know this. You know that a summer picnic is a better bet than a winter one, but that the weather on the day of the summer picnic could be wet, while that on the day of the winter picnic could be pleasant.

Getting climate and weather mixed up can create confusion: another famous writer, Michael Crichton (who wrote *Jurassic Park* and *Twister*), was doing just that when he wondered how scientists can claim that the climate is changing when they can't get weather forecasts right. Day-to-day weather may be very unpredictable, as we all know, but over years and decades the ups and downs in temperature, wind, and rain can be seen to be part of a stable and predictable pattern; that pattern is what we call climate.

Because climate is a pattern that reveals itself only over many years, you can't look at climate up close; you have to see the big picture. A single bit of weather—an extra-hot summer month or an unusually fierce storm—tells you as much about climate as the trunk of a single tree tells you about the whole forest. But a STRING of hot summers or a rise in the number and ferocity of storms **over several years** could show that the big picture—the long-term pattern of climate—is shifting, and that climate **is** changing.

That is what's happening to the earth right now. The long-term records of weather all over the world (see "How Do We Know That the Climate Is Changing?," page 25) show that the pattern isn't the same as it was one hundred or even fifty years ago. The earth is undergoing climate change. Overall, the planet is getting hotter, which is why some people call what's happening "global warming" or "global heating." But the earth's increasing temperature could affect all sorts of aspects of the climate—rainfall patterns, winds, and storms—so I'm going to use the term "climate change." It seems to be the most commonly used label these days anyhow.

The other term you might come across that's used to describe what's happening to our planet is "the greenhouse effect." It's worth understanding this one, because it actually tells you something about what causes climate change/global warming/global heating.

The greenhouse effect isn't a bad thing; without it we'd be like the moon, boiling when the sun's up and colder than a freezer after sunset, with an average temperature of 0°F(−18°C)! But, unlike the moon, we have an atmosphere, which stops us from getting too hot or too cold. Earth's atmosphere, along with its clouds and dust, *reflects* some of the sun's light straight back to space, so this light never has a chance to heat us. The remaining sunlight makes it to ground level and is absorbed by the earth's surface, which then heats up. The atmosphere also *traps* some of this heat, soaks it up, and then radiates it out again, sending some of it back out into space and some down to the earth's surface. Without an atmosphere, all that heat would be lost straight back into space, so the moment the sun went down, we'd be freezing cold again. This balance of keeping heat in and letting heat out is how the atmosphere keeps us comfortably cozy. (This isn't the way a greenhouse works, but the atmosphere and greenhouse glass both keep what's underneath them warm, so the name has stuck.)

The bad news is that the balance of heating and cooling has been upset. The atmosphere today is trapping more heat than it is losing. In other words, we now have a bigger greenhouse effect than we need, and it's making the earth hotter and changing our climate.

As the earth's climate gets hotter, deserts could expand.

Mark Maslin

Earth-Watching: Interview

Dr. Don Grainger studies clouds, smoke, dust, and air pollution—in fact, any tiny particles or droplets that float around in the atmosphere and might affect how much, or how little, of the sun's energy gets reflected back into space. Measuring these floating particles and droplets—known as aerosols—is hard from ground level, so Don and his team from the Department of Atmospheric, Oceanic and Planetary Physics at Oxford University do it from space, using satellites.

Dr. D. G. Richards

"We use two kinds of satellites," Don explains, "geostationary ones that stay in orbit over the same point 35,786 kilometers [22,300 miles] above the earth's surface, and polar orbit satellites that follow a path like a giant Hula-hoop 780 kilometers [485 miles] up."

NASA

Neither kind can take pictures of the whole earth at once, but they build a picture up from a series taken as they scan the surface. The pictures get beamed down to Earth and travel via the Internet to Don's computer (next to the two stuffed kiwi birds in his office). Analyzing the pictures—which are taken using both visible light and infrared (heat)—shows not only where the aerosols are, but what they are made of and how much light and heat they are reflecting. Don can monitor how the pollution from cities and factories builds up and then disperses, or how the smoke from forest fires mixes with clouds and changes the way they reflect light.

The photographs show the surface of the earth too—both the land and the sea—and the pictures taken using infrared allow Don and his team to monitor the temperature of the surface.

"Sea surface temperatures can be used to understand ocean currents, and this could improve our short-term forecasting of climate change."

The pictures show changes in land use too. Monitoring how much forest gets cut down or how deserts are spreading is very difficult from the ground, but this information can be seen much more clearly on a satellite picture. Don tells me:

"Andy, one of my students, recently showed me new estimates of deforestation rates in the Amazon derived from satellite images."

Here's a photo of Brazilian rain forest taken from a satellite. The brown areas on the left are deforested.

This matters because forests have a particularly important role to play in climate change (see "Keeping Gaia Green," page 142).

Although satellite images are used in weather forecasting—we've probably all seen them on TV weather broadcasts—their value to scientists like Don is in allowing them to look at the bigger picture and monitor the planet in the long term:

"Our expectations of climate change are based on computer models of how the Earth-atmosphere system works," says Don. "Satellite images can be used to help us understand these processes."

A composite image of the aerosol level in the atmosphere

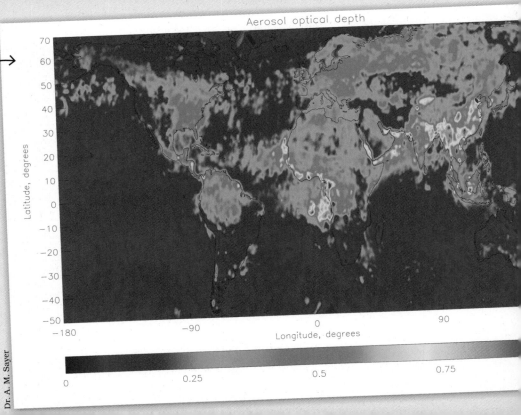

Dr. A. M. Sayer

AATSR False colour 20080611

An image colored to help show cloud structure

Dr. G. E. Thomas

In other words, what Don's work does is show what the earth's climate is really doing, not what the computer models expect it to do!

Don and his team would like to understand more about how aerosol pollution is changing the climate, but it will take a new generation of satellite technology to get to grips with the problem properly. In the meantime, there are moments when satellites simply show something wonderful:

"My favorite images are the long parallel lines of clouds caused by the atmosphere bouncing up and down over large mountain ranges."

> # "The ice is melting earlier and quicker. I'm worried for my future — the future of my generation."

LUDY PUDLUK

(An Inuit who has lived in the Arctic all his life, Ludy was a politician before retiring and devoting his time to campaigning for climate change.)

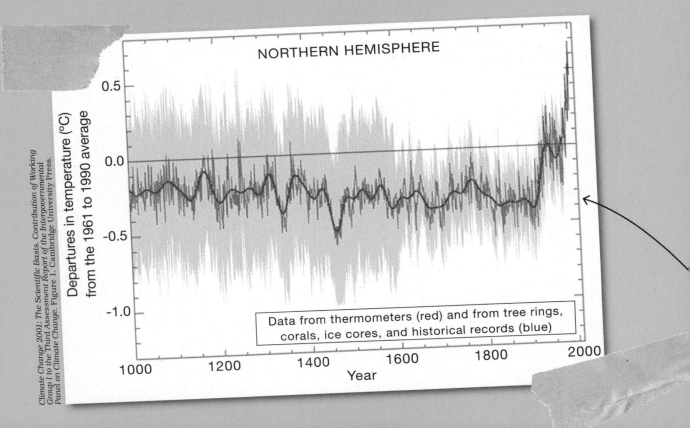

Climate Change 2001: The Scientific Basis. Contribution of Working Group I to the Third Assessment Report of the Intergovernmental Panel on Climate Change. Figure 1. Cambridge University Press.

NORTHERN HEMISPHERE

Departures in temperature (°C) from the 1961 to 1990 average

Data from thermometers (red) and from tree rings, corals, ice cores, and historical records (blue)

Year

How Do We Know That the Climate Is Changing?

If I were writing this in February in New York, I'd have to be wearing two pairs of socks, three sweaters, and a thick pair of jeans. Meanwhile, my brother in Melbourne, Australia, would probably be out in his yard in a bathing suit and a sun hat. If the temperature can be so different in different parts of the world, how can anyone tell what the whole planet is doing?

The answer is by using **averages**. If you measure the temperature in different parts of the globe—the cold parts, the warm parts, the medium parts— all through the year, then take an average of them all, it gives an average temperature for the whole planet.

This turns out to be about the same as on a coolish day in spring in Seattle, around 57°F (14°C). Or at least that is what it **used** to be.

People all over the world have been keeping records of temperatures for a very long time—in some places for more than four hundred years. Long before humans came along with thermometers, the planet itself kept a record of its temperature in the patterns of growth in trees and corals and in the ice of glaciers and polar ice caps. Modern climate scientists have taken a very careful look at these records and, using only the most reliable ones, have put them together with modern temperature measurements to see what the average temperature of the earth has been doing for the past one thousand years and more. Plotted onto a graph (see opposite), they show there's a bit of an

The "hockey stick" graph

up-and-down pattern in the earth's temperature year to year, but overall the graph is shaped like a hockey stick. What the now-famous "hockey stick" graph shows (even if you aren't a graphs kind of person) is that since about 1900 the earth's average temperature has been creeping up, and it is now rising faster than at any time since humans started measuring things. It's risen 1°F (0.5°C) since 1970, bringing the average global temperature today to about 58°F.

Across the world, **snow and ice** are disappearing. In the Arctic, the summer sea-ice cover is less than 80% of what it was in the 1970s. Glaciers, massive rivers of ancient ice, are melting faster than ever before, in the Arctic, in the Antarctic, and on mountaintops around the world; the glaciers that gave Glacier Bay National Park in Alaska its name will almost certainly be gone by 2030.

With so much melting going on, the SEA LEVEL is rising. This is tricky to measure—what with tides and waves and so on—but scientists agree that since 1900, world sea levels have gone up by almost eight inches, and they are now rising faster than ever before.

The warmer the planet, the warmer its oceans get (this adds to sea-level rise too, because water expands as it warms). Warm oceans are what drive tropical storms, and the frequency and ferocity of tropical storms—cyclones and hurricanes—seems to be increasing, particularly in the North Atlantic.

Temperature doesn't change on its own. It affects wind and rainfall, and there is evidence from across the globe that these are changing too. In Western Australia, rainfall has been dropping for fifty years, and there's now

Angelika Renner (UEA/BAS)

⬆ Ice floes in the
Antarctic, where
in some places the
ice is melting faster
than ever before

◀ As the planet warms,
summers could become hotter
and drier, making forest fires
more frequent.

30% less water in streams and rivers than in the 1970s. Southern Spain is getting drier too, while in northern Europe and North America, extreme downpours are more frequent.

If you aren't convinced by human measurements and observations, there is plenty of evidence that animals and plants are already reacting to climate change—much faster than human governments. Most species have a range of temperatures that they prefer to live within, and many of them are having to move to find that comfort zone. In 2003 a huge study of 1,700 different species showed that since 1950 they have moved on average almost four miles (six km) nearer the poles every ten years. Mountain species have moved twenty feet higher every decade. They don't read newspapers or watch TV, but their behavior is a clear sign that the earth's climate is changing.

Plants and animals are already reacting to climate change. By 2050 more than a third of all species could be extinct.

Don Becker (becker@usgs.gov), U.S. Geological Survey

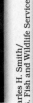

Charles H. Smith/
U.S. Fish and Wildlife Service

Don Becker, U.S. Geological Survey

Living in a Changed Climate: Interviews

Dr. Mohamed Ali lives in the Maldives, a country of 1,200 tiny coral islands. He feels the effects of climate change every day:

"We people of the Maldives have relied on our traditional calendar, the Nakaiy system, to predict the seasons and know when weather will be good for travel, for fishing. But now if I use Nakaiy to plan to travel to outer islands, it doesn't help—the weather turns rough and strange. Unpredictable weather is the main complaint now from farmers and fishermen."

But "strange," unseasonal weather is the least of their problems. Most of the islands are less than three feet above sea level. With sea level rising at just under half an inch a year, the Maldives will be gone in a century, and long before that, the islands will be uninhabitable. Already people are leaving as the salty ocean taints soil and freshwater supplies, making farming impossible, and storms regularly flood whole islands.

"These islands are so fragile, so vulnerable," says Dr. Ali, "but all we can do is protect our local environment—the mangroves and reefs that protect our islands. The rest is beyond our control. We can only ask the international community to cut greenhouse-gas emissions, and allow us to become climate refugees and give us access to land in industrial countries."

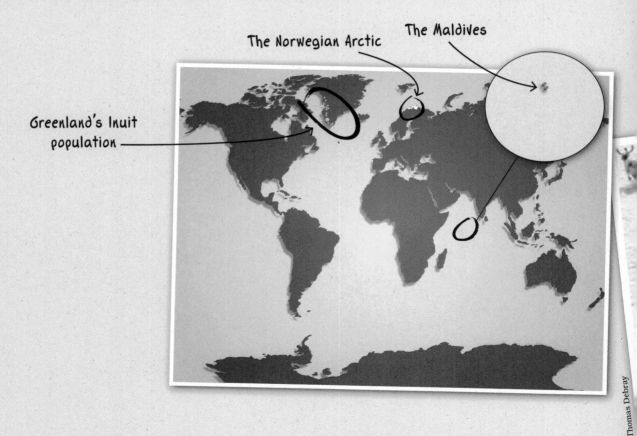

The Norwegian Arctic

The Maldives

Greenland's Inuit population

Olav Mathis Eira is a reindeer herder. For thousands of years his people, the Sami, have lived by herding the reindeer of the Norwegian Arctic, relying on their knowledge of the Arctic climate and landscape to find good grazing for their animals, even in the deepest winter snows. But the Arctic climate is changing twice as fast as anywhere else on Earth, and that makes finding lichen to eat harder and harder for Olav's animals:

"There are a lot of starving reindeer in some years,"
he says.

The Sami have moved with the times. They live in modern houses and have cars and washing machines like other twenty-first-century Europeans, but their livelihood and their culture depend on reindeer.

"If reindeer herding disappears, it will have a devastating effect," says Olav. "Climate change is threatening the entire Sami people."

Reindeer on the hills of Frøyningsfjellet, Norway

Ice melting in the Arctic is seriously affecting the Inuit way of life.

Mark Maslin

Farther north still, Inuit people all around the Arctic are feeling the effects of global warming. **Aqqaluk Lynge,** leader of Greenland's Inuit population, says:

"Climate change is not just a theory to us in the Arctic; it is a stark and dangerous reality."

Like the Sami, the Inuit face the destruction of their way of life and culture:

"Our ecosystem will be transformed, with tragic results," says Aqqaluk. "What will become of the Inuit? Climate change in the Arctic isn't just an environmental issue with unwelcome economic consequences. It's a matter of individual and cultural survival. It's a human issue. The Arctic is our home and homeland." And, Aqqaluk warns, "The serious consequences affecting my people today will affect your people tomorrow."

" **Doesn't global warming cause climate change? There's a link between the two but I'm not too sure what it is.** "

Member of the public, interviewed as part of a British government report on public understanding of climate change

(Actually, this person understands it slightly better than he thinks he does.)

What's Causing Climate Change?

To answer this question, we need to start by removing the **"change"** and ask, **"What causes climate?"** This is a HUGE question, and scientists are still working out the details, but here are the basics. The sun is the most important cause of climate. Without its energy, the earth would be a cold, dead piece of rock. The sun shines on our planet and warms it up. But it doesn't warm it equally. Because the earth is a sphere, sunlight hits both ends—the North and South poles—at a slant, spreading its energy more thinly there than on the tropics. This helps make the Arctic and Antarctic cold and the tropics hot. Also, the earth doesn't stand up straight as it goes around the sun; it's tilted, so for six months the north half gets the most sun and for the other six months the south half does, giving us winter and summer.

This unequal warming has another big climate effect: it gives us winds and ocean currents. Air rises as it gets warm, and cold air rushes in underneath to fill the space and—presto—produces wind! A similar thing happens in the oceans: warm water expands, flowing over the surface, while cold water sinks. So, with some parts of the planet getting more warmed up than others, there are risings and sinkings of air and water all the time, stirring the atmosphere and the oceans like giant hands. These stirrings set up planetwide patterns of winds, which move clouds and rain around the earth, and a vast global plumbing system of ocean currents, which cool some regions and warm others, helping to give each region its distinctive climate. Britain, for example, has a much warmer climate than it should have, given how far north it is, because of the warming effects of the North Atlantic Drift current that goes past its west coast. The color of the earth's surface also has an effect on how much the sun warms any piece of it. Dark areas, or to give them their proper scientific label, areas with a low ALBEDO, like seas and forests, soak up the sun's warmth. Light areas, areas with a high albedo, especially the bright-white polar ice caps, bounce the sun's rays straight back to space, so they never warm us (try going out on a sunny day with a black T-shirt on, then a white T-shirt, to see for yourself how this works). The high albedo of the polar ice caps has a cooling effect on the whole planet.

Oceans and forests—the dark, low-albedo areas—tend to warm us up. But that warmth gives us another important part of our climate—rain, because water evaporates from warm seas and moist forests to form clouds. Clouds can be climate coolers: they cool whatever area they formed from—just as sweat cools your skin as it evaporates—and when they cause rain, they cool whatever area they fall on. Clouds have a high albedo, so clouds high up over a forest or an ocean can turn a source of warming into a source of cooling. But clouds can also be climate warmers, holding heat close to the earth's surface like a blanket. In fact, the heating and cooling effects of clouds are among the things that climate scientists are struggling to understand.

It's complicated, isn't it? So, for a minute, let's really simplify things and think about climate like a central heating system:

◉ Sun provides heat (like the furnace of a central heating system);

◉ Winds and ocean currents soak up the sun's heat and move it around the planet (like pipes and radiators);

◎ The albedo of ice, snow, and some clouds cools us down (like uninsulated doors, windows, and roofs);

◎ Low clouds keep heat from escaping (like the insulation in an attic).

Working together, these parts of the central heating system give us the pattern of climate for the planet—cold poles, hot tropics, and everything else somewhere in between. But the factor that controls *how* cold and *how* hot the poles and tropics are—the thermostat for the whole planet's central heating system—is the atmosphere. And the setting of that thermostat depends on the greenhouse effect.

Now, the really important thing to know about the greenhouse effect is that it is created by gases that make up less than 2% of the earth's atmosphere. The most important of these "greenhouse gases" are water vapor, carbon dioxide (CO_2), and methane. They form a tiny part of the atmosphere, but, like the drop of red paint that turns a can of white paint pink, these greenhouse gases have a big, big, **BIG** effect: if their concentration rises, even a little, then the atmosphere traps more of the sun's warmth.

And that is just what has happened: CO_2 levels are 30% higher than they were two hundred years ago, and methane levels have more than doubled since those pre-industrial times. Water vapor has increased too, because the warmer the earth becomes, the more water vapor there is in the air. All in all, the earth's thermostat has been turned up.

We can't see or smell what's happened to the atmosphere all around us, but it's happened all the same, and that little change in the mixture of our air is what is causing climate change.

Air Monitor: Interview

Michael Trudeau works for the U.S. government's National Oceanic and Atmospheric Administration (NOAA) in Colorado. He's one of many scientists all over the world who monitor the chemistry of the atmosphere.

"I spend most of my days in shorts and sandals, sitting at my desk," he says, "imagining how human activities might influence greenhouse gases and the earth's climate.

Hawaii   Colorado

Michael Trudeau

Right now, I'm working on a computer model that calculates atmospheric concentration of methane."

Methane is the next most important greenhouse gas after CO_2. It comes from wetlands, rice paddies, and the digestive systems of cows and sheep, but also from the burning of forests, the mining of fossil fuels, and the landfill sites where we dump our trash. Even though there's less of it in the atmosphere than of CO_2, its greenhouse effect is sixty times more potent, and there's growing scientific evidence that it could cause big, fast warming. Mike explains:

"Small increases in global temperatures could increase methane emissions from wetlands and release methane from under the sea. An increase in the concentration of such a potent greenhouse gas could produce sudden warming."

NOAA employee Paul Fukumura is monitoring changes in greenhouse gases by taking air samples at the Mauna Loa Observatory in Hawaii.

Mike's computer models need accurate information to work on, so Mike measures how much methane is in the atmosphere with a device that uses a laser beam:

"It works on the principle that methane absorbs certain wavelengths of light," Mike explains. "It's like shining a light through a cup of coffee: the stronger the brew, the less light makes it through the cup."

Scientists are paying a lot of attention to methane right now, because while CO_2 stays in the atmosphere for a hundred years—making any change in CO_2 emissions slow to show an effect—methane stays in the air for just nine years.

"So," Mike says, "if we change the amount we emit, we'll produce a change in the atmosphere on shorter timescales."

This means that cutting methane emissions—through changes in how we dispose of our garbage and how we farm the land—could put a relatively fast-acting brake on global warming.

"But before governments can sit down and draft agreements about emissions," says Mike, "greenhouse-gas inventories for each nation need to be understood."

Mike's work is helping supply that information about who emits which greenhouse gases and how much.

"The real questions," Mike concludes, "are how bad are we going to let things get through our inaction, and what kind of world do we want to pass on to our children?"

> " It's true we've had higher CO_2 levels before. But then, of course, we also had dinosaurs. "
>
> *NOAA scientist*

(NOAA, the U.S. National Oceanic and Atmospheric Administration, researches and monitors everything about the sea and the air. It's a very serious scientific organization, which doesn't really make jokes; maybe that's why this scientist, interviewed by author Elizabeth Kolbert for her book *Field Notes from a Catastrophe*, didn't give a name.)

But Hasn't the Climate Always Changed?

The short answer to this question is "yes." The earth is seriously ancient—around 4.5 billion years old—and in its long life it's been a lot hotter and a lot colder than it is now. In just the last couple of hundred million years—pretty recently as far as the earth is concerned—its climate has switched from hothouse to icehouse. Around 130 million years ago, when dinosaurs were stomping around the planet, there were no ice caps and it was warm enough for tropical plants to grow near the poles. But about 50 million years ago the earth began to cool down, and for about the last 13 million years it's been an icehouse, with two frozen poles and more than twenty ice ages (more correctly called "glacial periods") in the last 3 million years, which covered Europe and North America in a layer of ice more than a mile thick.

If the earth's climate has changed naturally so much in the past, why should we be worried about climate change now? Well, two reasons. The first is that all of human civilization—agriculture, cities, art, science, hot baths, iPods, and jet planes—has developed in a nice, balmy interglacial (that's the warm period of time between icy glacial periods), which has given the earth 10,000 years of easy, stable climate. There have been some variations—warm periods and cold snaps lasting a few hundred years—which were too small to count as major changes to the global climate but can be linked to crop failures, famine, mass migration, and even the collapse of entire civilizations. So we know that even quite mild climate change can be pretty destructive.

The second reason is that the more scientists find out about why and how climate changed in the past, the more it confirms that we could be in for a hot future because of increasing levels of greenhouse gases in our atmosphere today.

That isn't to say that greenhouse gases have been the only thing involved in past climate change; on the timescale of the earth's long life, there have been many changes in the planetary central heating system. The positions of the windows, doors, radiators, and piping have altered because of continental drift. This is the slow waltzing of the continents, which happens over tens of millions of years. It changes the position of the land; makes seas; blocks or opens the flow of heat-carrying ocean currents; and influences the formation of polar ice caps, which can form only when there is land at, or near, the poles. One of the causes of the shift from dino-hothouse to icehouse was Antarctica breaking away from the other continents, allowing ocean currents to flow all around it and cool it down. Over millions of years, isolated down there at the South Pole, it cooled enough to freeze. Having a giant ice cube at the bottom of the world cooled the whole planet down.

The heat we get out of the boiler, too, has varied over time. The amount of energy we get from the sun peaks slightly every eleven years with the activity of sunspots (dark spots on the sun's surface) and cycles. It also changes because of regular variations in the earth's orbit around the sun, which can take tens or even hundreds of thousands of years. Three million years ago, with the top and bottom of the world already in the freezer and the whole planet on the cool side, the "lows" and "highs" of these variations almost certainly helped to turn ice ages on and off.

But this isn't the whole story. Research has shown that every time there has been a climate shift, there has also been a change in the level of greenhouse gases in the atmosphere. Fifty-five million years ago, when the earth was already in a hothouse phase, there was a sudden spike in levels of greenhouse gases. It's too long ago for us to be able to say which gases and exactly how fast their levels went up, but the likely candidate is methane, released from stores under the sea by the already high temperatures. Right afterward, the earth's temperature shot up by 9°F (5°C) over about a thousand years—a blink of an eye in Earth-history terms.

But soon after that mega heat wave, greenhouse-gas levels began falling again, and Earth began to cool—30 million years before Antarctica had broken away to planet-cooling isolation at the South Pole and not linked to any of the cycles in the sun's input. Greenhouse gases went on falling and Earth went on cooling, so when Antarctica did at last break away, Earth was already on the way to the icehouse.

Much more recently, the cycles of glacial periods and interglacials also seemed linked with greenhouse-gas levels, as well as with sun cycles. Ever since this freeze-and-thaw pattern began around 3 million years ago, there have been more than twenty glacial periods and interglacials. Every time CO_2 and methane levels fell (CO_2 by about a third and methane by about a half), there was a glacial period, and every time they rose again, there was an interglacial.

The big question is, of course, did changes in CO_2 and other greenhouse-gas levels **cause** global temperatures to change? It's hard to be absolutely sure about the sudden temperature change of 55 million years ago—although it seems very likely. The evidence from the ice ages is much clearer. It shows that CO_2 levels rose AND THEN temperatures rose. It isn't a precise recipe—so many spoonfuls of CO_2 give so many degrees of rising temperature—and it's obvious that other factors have been involved too, but it's pretty clear that greenhouse gases, and CO_2 in particular, have played a major role in driving climate change and controlling the earth's thermostat.

We now have the highest levels of greenhouse gases in the atmosphere for 800,000 years. If those levels of greenhouse gases go on rising at their current rate, by 2050 they'll be higher than they've been for several million years. And from all we know of what's happened in the past, that will mean a much hotter future.

Measuring the Climate of the Past: Interview

Louise Sime

Nerilie Abram is a paleoclimatologist— someone who studies what climate was like in the past. She's been busy drilling holes in the Antarctic to get long cylinders of ice—called cores—tens of thousands of years old.

Paleoclimatologists like Nerilie are detectives, build- ing a picture of what climate used to be like using clues of all sorts: the fossils of plants and animals; the shells of plankton and grains of pollen in mud at the bottoms of lakes and seas; tree rings; layers in rock; radioactive materials—all these provide pieces of the picture. But for Nerilie, ice cores are the best:

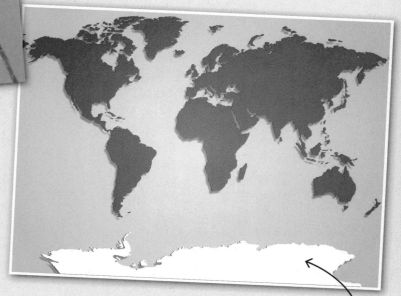

The Antarctic

Nerilie exploring a crevasse in the ice near the British Antarctic Survey base at Rothera

"Ice cores let you put together all the different parts of the puzzle," she says. "There's no other kind of record that can tell you so much about so many different parts of the climate system."

The amount of salt in the cores shows how hard the wind was blowing off the sea, so researchers can reconstruct how stormy the climate was; volcanic dust in the cores shows when volcanoes erupted; and bands in the ice show where it melted and thawed again as the temperature rose and fell. Ice can even tell researchers what the temperature was like elsewhere on the planet when the ice was formed. Nerilie explains:

"Heavier isotopes (forms) of water take more energy to lift out of the ocean and blow to the Antarctic to make snow. So when the climate is warmer, there are more heavy isotopes in the snow falling on Antarctica. It's a chemical signal of climate, locked in as the snow turns to ice."

Perhaps best of all, ice cores contain little bubbles of ancient air:

Ice-core drilling camp on top of
James Ross Island, which was home
to seven scientists for two months

Nerilie Abram

"These are the only direct way we have of knowing exactly what the composition of the atmosphere was in the past—including greenhouse-gas concentrations."

Nerilie and the team from the British Antarctic Survey in Cambridge, England, were drilling on the mountainous James Ross Island, a part of the Antarctic Peninsula. The ice there is more than 1,000 feet thick, and around 25,000 years old at the bottom. They drilled "cores" in sequence from the surface ("now") to the bottom

Nerilie Abram

The barrel of the ice-core drill with an ice sample inside

("25,000 years ago"), then packed them onto a refrigerated ship to be taken back to Cambridge.

Nerilie's latest ice cores are in the lab now, and she hopes they are going to provide answers to some important questions:

"The Antarctic Peninsula, where we were working, is warming faster than the rest of Antarctica. Our ice cores will tell us whether this has happened before and how it's related to temperature change. They'll help us to work out how fast the Antarctic ice sheets might melt in future, and how fast sea levels might rise."

Nerilie may spend her days looking at an ancient ice cube, but she definitely has her mind on the future:

"Scientists are no longer trying to convince people that global warming is happening," she says. "We're trying to work out what it will be like, how to plan for it, and how to prevent the worst-case scenario."

Everything for the ice-core drilling camp was brought to the site by two Lynx helicopters operating off the Royal Navy ship HMS Endurance. At the end of the project, everything was removed again, so that the site was left in a pristine condition.

"The use of solar energy has not been opened up because the oil industry does not own the sun."

RALPH NADER

(Ralph Nader is a lawyer and campaigner who has spent his life standing up for the interests of ordinary people and the environment. He was one of the first people to call for a shift to renewable forms of energy and an end to environmental pollution — and he has run for President of the United States four times!)

Is Climate Change Our Fault?

We know that our climate is changing, and we can be pretty sure it's because levels of greenhouse gases, CO_2 in particular, have risen. But we also know that levels of greenhouse gases went up and down like a monkey on a ladder long before humans were around to influence them. How do we know that this time it's our fault?

One way is to take a good look at the natural sources of greenhouse gases in our atmosphere. Unlike continental drift or changes in the sun's energy, the atmosphere—the earth's thermostat—is actually controlled by life itself. The vast web of living things—microbes, plants, and animals—interacts with sea, air, and rock to form a single interdependent system, which behaves as if it were one giant body. This mega system was given the name **Gaia** by James Lovelock more than thirty years ago. Gaia was a pretty wacky idea back then, but now most scientists accept that it is a useful way to think about how our planet works. It's also much quicker to write than "vast web of living things," etc.

Gaia creates our atmosphere and is constantly soaking up and releasing greenhouse gases. For example, every time you or any other animal on the planet breathes out (respiration), CO_2 is put into the air, but every time a plant grows, it takes some CO_2 out of the air and uses it (photosynthesis). On a longer timescale, the oceans, rocks, and soil take CO_2 out of the air too:

CO_2 dissolves in oceans, and tiny plants and animals take up some of it and make their shells with it; when they die, their shells sink to the seabed and the CO_2 they contain is locked away for thousands, or even millions, of years. Rocks and soil take CO_2 out of the air by reacting with it and turning it into a different chemical—a process called *weathering,* which is speeded up by plants and microbes on the surface of rocks and in the soil. And there are similar to-ings and fro-ings for methane and water vapor.

Scientists have added up all these natural sources of greenhouse gases, now and in the past, and fed them into a computer model to see if they create the changes in climate that we're experiencing in the real world (see "If It's Only a Few Degrees, What Difference Will It Make?," page 61). What they've found is that the natural sources of CO_2 and other greenhouse gases add up nicely to account for the real ups and downs in global temperature in the PAST, but they don't match the temperatures that have been measured for the last fifty to one hundred years. Only when the scientists add in the CO_2 and greenhouse gases from **our** activities—our gas-, coal-, and oil-burning from all our cars, factories, power stations, and farms—does the math add up. The only way to explain why there is so much greenhouse gas in the atmosphere is that it's because of **us**.

Normally, Gaia balances the processes that put CO_2 and other greenhouse gases into the atmosphere with the processes that take them out. This balancing act isn't perfect and it doesn't work very fast, but over the billions of years of the earth's history, it's been a pretty robust system. It works through a series of what's called negative-feedback systems. For example, if CO_2 levels rise, then so does temperature; plant growth and weathering are boosted, removing CO_2 from the atmosphere, and so CO_2 levels drop again and temperature follows. This is part of the trigger for glacial periods and interglacials, and it is the system that returned greenhouse gases to a more normal level after that massive spike 55 million years ago.

Mostly Gaia keeps greenhouse gases, and therefore the thermostat setting, at about the same level for tens of thousands of years at a time. But if the feedback systems are hugely overloaded in either direction, the thermostat can change to a different setting. For example, at the start of the dino-hothouse period, large amounts of volcanic activity over hundreds of thousands of years loaded the atmosphere with so much greenhouse gas that the thermostat switched to "hotter." After the dino-hothouse period, weathering of the rocks of the newly formed Himalayas caused such a large, long-term fall in CO_2 levels that the earth's thermostat turned to "cooler."

There's plenty of evidence to show that some of Gaia's negative feedbacks are under severe pressure. For example, rising sea temperatures are slowing the growth of marine plants; this is a double whammy, because not only does it reduce the amount of CO_2 they soak up, but also it reduces the formation of cooling clouds, which algae help to form by pumping cloud-seeding droplets of chemicals into the air. So seas get warmer, and these effects get worse. Cutting down tropical forests is another case of our knocking a hole in a useful feedback system (we're destroying about fifty soccer fields' worth every hour). Dead trees release all the CO_2 they collected in their lifetime and, of course, can't grow and soak up any more CO_2. That CO_2 stays in the atmosphere,

NOAA News Photo/FEMA

Volcanic eruptions have had a big effect on Earth's climate in the past but have little to do with the global warming that is happening now.

again driving the temperature up and causing droughts that threaten remaining forests, and so on.

There's no volcanic eruption we can blame for our current greenhouse-gas levels, and there are no emerging Himalayan mountains to soak them up, so we can't say this situation is Gaia's fault and we can't hope that she'll get us out of it. We have overloaded our atmosphere with greenhouse gases, damaged the living systems that might help take them out again, and turned our planet's thermostat to "hotter." Not very bright, is it?

Who's the Climate-Change Bad Guy?

Deciding who's the biggest CO_2 bad guy isn't easy. CO_2 hangs around for about a century and gets pretty well mixed into the whole atmosphere, so any particular country's CO_2 doesn't just sit like a guilty cloud over the top of it, ready to be measured; the amount of it has to be calculated from how much fossil fuel has been used. Also, because CO_2 lasts so long, it's not just the countries pumping out the CO_2 now that have caused climate change, it's the countries that were doing it fifty years ago. And whose CO_2 emission is it if one country's industry creates emissions while making stuff for another country to use? (Just think of all the things we buy that say "Made in China.") Overall we know that about four-fifths of the extra CO_2 in the atmosphere comes from our industrial way of life, but the other fifth is the result of deforestation (see "Keeping Gaia Green," page 142), so some countries that don't burn much fossil fuel could turn out to be top CO_2 bad guys if we looked at their record of cutting forests down—Brazil and Indonesia, for instance.

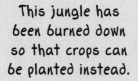

This jungle has been burned down so that crops can be planted instead.

Jami Dwyer

A LINEUP OF THE WORST OFFENDERS

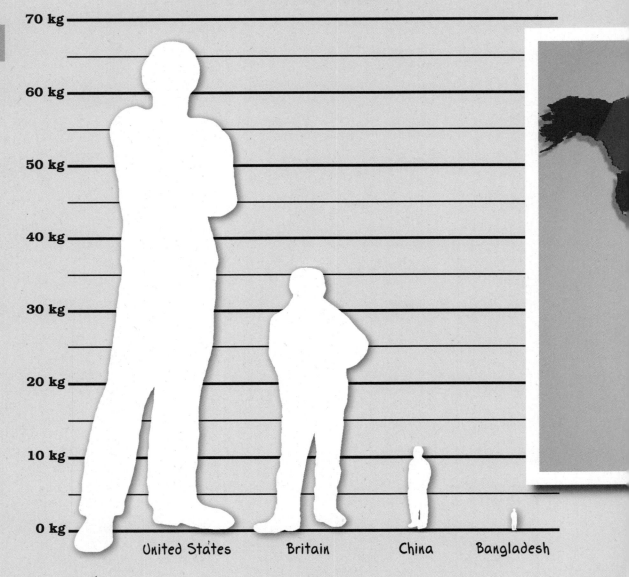

70 kg
60 kg
50 kg
40 kg
30 kg
20 kg
10 kg
0 kg

United States   Britain   China   Bangladesh

Daily greenhouse-gas emissions for each person in the United States are the equivalent of 67 kg (148 lbs.) CO_2, as much as for six people in China, two in Britain, and twenty-seven in Bangladesh.

WORLDWIDE CO$_2$ EMISSIONS PER PERSON

most per
person

least per
person

" We are going to see a world in which calamities — famines, great loss of life, big storms — are much more common. . . . Global warming is the biggest problem facing us this century, bigger even than the problems of global terrorism. "

LORD OXBOROUGH

(i.e., BIG, BIG BOSS)

Chief Executive Officer, Shell

(Yes, that's Shell, the oil company.)

If It's Only a Few Degrees, What Difference Will It Make?

From what we can tell about past climate change, a few degrees is all it takes to make a big difference. The earth 7°F (4°C) colder than it is now was in the grip of an ice age, while when it was on average just 9°F (5°C) warmer than now, it was a dino-hothouse with palm trees at the poles. Less than 2°F of cooling seven hundred years ago brought on the "Little Ice Age," with crop failure, famine, and plague across Europe. We know that, right now, the 1°F rise in average global temperatures is already having a big impact on the world—shrinking ice caps and glaciers, raising sea levels, and causing floods, droughts, and shifts in the distribution of plants and animals.

One reason that even a small rise in average temperatures can have a big impact is that it can mean changes in the **highest** temperatures. The heat wave that hit Europe in the summer of 2003, for example, broke highest-temperature records in four countries and killed 50,000 people. In 1998 and 2002, the water temperature in the Pacific and Indian oceans also broke records, rising high enough to damage and even kill coral reefs. Although it's impossible to tie one specific weather event to global warming, the frequency of these extreme temperatures is increasing.

Another reason is that some places are warming faster than others. Temperatures in the Arctic have risen twice as much as on the rest of the planet. This is why Arctic ice is disappearing and the frozen-hard soils of the Arctic—the permafrost—are turning soggy, causing trees, houses, lakes, and roads to sink into the mud. Parts of Antarctica are also warming up faster than average: the temperature of the Antarctic Peninsula is rising by almost 1°F every ten years, so it's not so surprising that a Rhode Island–size piece of the Antarctic ice shelf broke up in 2002.

Polar regions are particularly sensitive to temperature change because it takes only a small rise in temperature to go from "freeze" to "thaw," and if our poles thaw, they won't be able to do the planet-cooling job that they do now, so Earth will get hotter still. This is the key to another reason relatively small changes in temperature can pack a big punch: they can trigger positive-feedback loops that speed up warming and make climate change worse. For example, melting ice caps mean a smaller area of bright white on the earth's surface, so albedo goes down, and there are more dark areas to soak up more of the sun's warmth, causing further rises in temperature and even more melting of the ice caps.

The hotter Earth gets, the more of these nasty loops we could get caught in.

Of course, the 1°F rise in global temperatures that has already happened isn't the end of our current climate change. Even if we stopped putting any more greenhouse gases into the air, the temperature would still go on rising, because the CO_2 we've already put into the atmosphere will hang around for almost a hundred years. Right now, human activities are putting CO_2 and other greenhouse gases into the atmosphere faster than ever before, so we'll get warmer still.

One way to figure out how much hotter it might get and what that might mean for the earth's climate is to make a computer model of how things could pan out. Computer models of climate change include absolutely everything that science knows about climate and how it works: measurements of temperature, rain, wind, and ocean currents; the impact of forests, deserts, and volcanoes; the variations in the energy input from the sun; the amount of greenhouse gases in the atmosphere; even the effect of vapor trails from aircraft and pollution from cars and factories. Facts and figures are combined with the best information we have about how all these components fit together, and all of it is added to the computer mix. Then the models are run like an incredibly complicated computer game to show how climate might play out under different sets of conditions. The accuracy of the models is checked by "hindcasting," or using a model to show how climate changed in the past. If a model is able to re-create a climate very close to what things were really like, then it can be used to predict what might happen in the future.

These are the sorts of models that the Intergovernmental Panel on Climate Change (IPCC—see Glossary, page 188) has used to try to predict how climate is going to change. What the panel has come up with is that over the next ninety years or so, the earth is going to warm up by 3°F–7°F (1.5°C–4.5°C). It's not that the models can't give a more accurate prediction of warming, it's just that different sets of information fed into the models give different answers. If, for example, we cut emissions of greenhouse gases, then the 3°F end of the range is more likely; if we go on increasing our emissions, as we are now, then we'll wind up at the top end of the range;

and if we do nothing either way, we'll be in the middle—an increase of about five degrees.

This sounds pretty modest, until you look at the last time the Earth was five degrees hotter. That was three million years ago, and back then there was far less ice at the poles and the seas were 80 feet (25 m) deeper than they are now. A world five degrees hotter would be very different from the world we are used to. The best climate models for such a world predict droughts, floods, and rising sea levels. This will mean water shortages, crop failures, and famine, plus the spread of diseases like malaria: by 2080, 600 million more people could be facing starvation and 320 million more could suffer from malaria. Coastal cities like London and low-lying countries like the Netherlands could suffer frequent floods and start to drown in the rising seas. None of the predictions made by climate models about the five-degree-hotter world says, "All OK, just a bit warmer in the summer!"

A rise of more than five degrees takes us into the territory of nasty feedback loops that could accelerate climate change and make things even hotter.

Another danger sign is that computer models tend to assume that climate change happens in a nice smooth way, a bit more every year, when in reality the climate can change in fits and starts, so we could be in for some sudden shocks. What's more, some parts of the system are changing much faster than the models predicted—Arctic ice, for example, is disappearing more quickly than the models indicated it might.

And one more thing to remember: at the moment, greenhouse-gas emissions aren't going down or even staying the same; they are rising faster than ever before.

All in all, it's not looking good. But we do still have time to improve our prospects. The computer models show that the biggest temperature rises are likely **if we don't do anything about cutting the amount of greenhouse gases we put into the atmosphere.** Which means if we **DO** cut our emissions, we have a chance of keeping the temperature rises smaller. We can't keep climate change from happening, but we **CAN** slow it down, try to keep ourselves out of some of the worst feedback loops, and buy ourselves a bit more time to adapt to the problems it will present.

It won't be a picnic. There will be further rises in sea levels, more damaging storms, less predictable rain for our crops, fierce heat waves, and possibly some nasty climate surprises that we can't foresee. But if we cut our emissions, we stand a chance of keeping civilization together and holding on to some of our most important ecosystems, like the Amazon rain forest.

If we don't, we risk taking all the fun there is right out of the world.

Nasty Shocks and Tipping Points: Interview

"Think about what happens when you lean back in a chair," says **Tim Lenton,** Professor of Earth System Science at the University of East Anglia, in England. "You get to a certain point where a small nudge will send you falling backwards onto the floor. That is the tipping point, the boundary between one stable state—sitting up— and another—sprawled on the floor."

Tee Rogers—Hayden (UEA)

Toppling chairs may seem pretty far removed from climate change, but Tim and scientific colleagues from around the world think that parts of the earth's climate system could have tipping points just like a tilted chair:

Tim up a mountain, on a research trip in South Island, New Zealand

"Nudge the system past a certain point," Tim says, **"and a big change will start to occur."**

The things that Tim and his colleagues have identified as being vulnerable to this kind of change include ice sheets in Greenland and the Western Antarctic, the Atlantic thermohaline circulation (what's commonly referred to as the Gulf Stream—see Glossary, page 189), the Indian summer monsoon, and the Amazon rain forest. What this means is that if climate warms to even a little above the tipping point for these places, they could switch from one state to another—from frozen to melted, from flowing to not flowing, from rain to drought, from forest to grassland. And just as with a tipping chair, once they start to happen, these changes are irreversible.

What's more, passing one tipping point could trigger others, like a row of dominoes. For example, if the tipping point for melting the Greenland ice sheet was passed, the meltwater would stop the Atlantic thermohaline circulation; this in turn would keep warmer water in the Southern Ocean and speed up the melting of the West Antarctic ice sheet.

Courtesy of the U.S. Geological Society

Sea ice on the
Arctic Ocean

It's pretty important to know where these tipping points lie, so that we can make sure we don't allow the planet to warm up enough to go past them. Tim's research shows that on the approach to a tipping point, the thing that's about to tip behaves oddly—it changes in unusual ways. However, detecting these changes requires very detailed information about the thing—monsoon rains or ice sheet or ocean current—that could be about to tip. Says Tim:

"Unfortunately, we don't have a good record for many of the most vulnerable parts of the earth."

We might even have passed some tipping points already:

"We may have passed a tipping point for the Arctic sea ice," Tim says. "Soon it will reach a state where nearly all of it melts every summer. Arctic summers will be warmer, and the atmosphere's circulation patterns will change, so that the climate in northern Europe and North America will be affected."

Although identifying tipping points is hard, so far Tim's research suggests that we are several degrees away from many of the nasty ones—but that isn't a reason to relax:

"So far," he says, "there's been a lot of talk and very little action. It really needs a combination of individual action and bold global leadership to slow down climate change."

And it isn't a reason for Tim to be gloomy about his job, either:

"I have the best job in the world. I try to understand how planet Earth works as a whole system."

"**Who will have the courage in twenty-five years' time to tell their children, 'Yes, we could have solved this problem, but it was too expensive'?**"

HERMANN SCHEER
Social Democrat member of the German parliament and president of the European Association for Renewable Energy

(A man who sees the change to "greener" technologies as an economic opportunity, not a burden.)

What If the Scientists Have Made a Mistake, and We Waste Money Preparing for Something That Never Happens?

In 2007 the IPCC stated in its fourth report, "Human-induced warming of the climate is widespread."

In other words, the collective opinion of the world's most knowledgeable scientists is that there's no longer any doubt about the reality of global warming. So I almost didn't include this question, because there are very few people left in the world who still believe that climate change just isn't happening. But for the sake of that tiny percentage of human ostriches, I thought it deserved a place in this book.

There are two answers to this question, and they are both pretty short. The first is that the money wouldn't be wasted. Reducing our greenhouse-gas emissions to slow climate change means we'd be investing in fuel efficiency and more environmentally friendly ways of doing things. With fossil fuels — oil, coal, and gas — not to mention most other natural resources, slowly but surely running out and rapidly rising in price, this makes sound economic sense. Preparing for the impact of climate change we can't avoid, such as the effects of droughts, floods, and rising sea levels, will reduce the suffering of the world's poorest people, who are being hit by these problems right now.

Climate change is already happening, so waiting to see if more predictions come true before we take action is like staring into the glare of the headlights to see if the car will hit you. The longer we wait, the more expensive it's going to be to fix and the more unpleasant it will be to live through. The Stern Review, a big U.K. government report about how much climate change could cost the whole world, estimated that acting now to limit it would cost about 2% of the world's money every year. *Not* acting now, and having to cope with the worst effects later, could, in the worst-case scenario, end up costing 20% of the world's money every year.

Businesses all over the world are already working hard to cut their CO_2 and other greenhouse-gas emissions **because it saves them lots of money**. Insurance companies had to pay out five times more in 2008 than in 2006 mostly because of a big increase in "natural" disasters. They are calling on companies and governments to cut greenhouse-gas emissions and prepare for climate change now, so that floods, storms, and hurricanes don't eat all their profits in the future. (Though beware of companies who claim to be "green" or "sustainable" just to sell you something. Look up the term "greenwashing" online.)

The second answer is much shorter, and it's this:

What if the scientists are right, and we don't do anything?

Think about it. A world getting hotter and hotter; famine, floods, and chaos because nobody has prepared for climate change or tried to slow it down.

It's not a gamble any **SANE** person would take.

Columns and Rows

Surfing the Net I found a brilliant little video that explained the arguments about climate change and what we should do about it very simply in a table with two columns and two rows. Here is my summary:

CLIMATE CHANGE	WE DO EVERYTHING WE CAN TO STOP IT	WE DO NOTHING TO STOP IT
DOESN'T HAPPEN & Isn't a Big Deal	Oops, that means we wasted some money, so... -1	Well, that's no change, so... 0
DOES HAPPEN & Is a Big Deal	Lots of money and effort spent, but we save the world. That'd be a big plus for me, but to keep the skeptics happy... 0	Famine, chaos, disaster—how do you score that...? -3
	$= -1$	$= -3$
	(So that's money & effort spent needlessly)	(End of civilization as we know it!)

So we need to stop arguing about the rows and make sure we get the right column.

" I am nine years old, and even I know that global warming is very bad and dangerous to my future. If we can't stop polluting the air, we will all die. "

from NEW SCIENTIST magazine's
website comments board

" The global-warming scenario is pretty grim. I'm not sure I like the idea of polar bears under a palm tree. "

LENNY HENRY
comedian

(If nine-year-olds and comedians are worried, maybe we all should be!)

It's All Too Big and Scary, and There's Nothing I Can Do About It!

It *is* all big and scary, but I don't believe it's the big scariness that makes people feel there's nothing they can do. Humans have a good track record of tackling big, scary things, after all—just think of landing on the moon. No, I think the root of "there's nothing I can do about it" lies in the fact that climate change is so hard to get your head around. I mean, how can we little humans, down here, have an effect on something as vastly huge as the whole atmosphere, up there? And how can there be billions of tons of anything in the air, when air doesn't seem to weigh anything? You just can't picture it, can you?

So let's try to get some pictures in our heads that will help make climate change seem real enough to do something about. First, that "vastly huge" atmosphere. Instead of looking at it from down here, like shrimps looking up from the bottom of a rock pool, let's look at the earth from space, the

Here is what our beautiful planet looks like from space.

NASA

way the first moonwalkers did forty years ago. From the moon, the earth looks small enough to hold in your hand, a beautiful blue-and-white globe floating in the dead blackness. The atmosphere isn't vast and huge now; in fact, it's barely visible, just a wisp of blue, as thin as a layer of plastic wrap. Looking at the atmosphere like that, as a see-through veil that's almost not there at all, it's easier to understand how fragile it is and how it might be damaged by what humans do.

Now, go back down to Earth and stretch out your arms. Imagine a column of air with a base about the size of a picnic table resting on your outstretched arms, going up and up so that its top is seventy miles above you, where air turns into space. Move your arms up and down to jiggle your column a bit. It doesn't seem to weigh anything, because it is pressing on you equally in all directions, even from inside every cell in your body, but it *does* weigh something. In fact, your table-size column weighs about 20 tons. Which is just a little bit less than the weight of CO_2 and other greenhouse gases that you—and all you do, eat, and buy—put into the atmosphere every year: 27 tons.

So, now you can make a mental picture of the greenhouse gas that's getting into the atmosphere every year because of you. (If you lived in Quatar or Saudi Arabia you need to imagine a bigger column—one with a base more like a pool table—and if you lived in Bangladesh your column could almost fit on one hand.)

OK so far? Now scale it up, and imagine everybody in your family, then your school, then your town, each with their own columns of greenhouse gases above them. Tons and tons and tons of it, all going into that fragile, wispy atmosphere.

The great thing is that you can do something to protect the atmosphere from all that CO_2, because you have control over your column and you can start to take action right now, action that will make it smaller:

◉ Turn down the heater in your room and wear another sweater instead;

◉ turn off the air-conditioning and open a window instead;

◉ take the TV off standby and turn it right off by unplugging it.

Already your column has shrunk. And you can shrink other columns too—just tell people about their columns and how they can shrink them. Tell your government that you'd like them to help everyone with column-shrinking. You have a lot more power than you think.

Yes, whole countries will have to make huge cuts in the amount of greenhouse gases they put into the atmosphere; yes, oceans and forests will have to be protected so that Gaia's natural climate-balancing system is restored; and yes, it will be tens or hundreds of years before our atmosphere has completely recovered. But all that huge change starts with everyone taking responsibility for his or her own personal column of greenhouse gas. Big? Yes. Scary? Maybe. But let's do it anyway.

Making Sense of Carbon: Interview

Antony Turner/CarbonSense

"If carbon dioxide were purple," says **Antony Turner**, "the sky would now be a different color. But CO$_2$ is invisible, and because we haven't seen it, we haven't paid it enough attention."

Having spent half his career working as a businessman in engineering companies, Antony is now devoting all his time to making sure we all start paying attention to CO$_2$.

His company, CarbonSense, helps businesses and individuals see the reality of their carbon footprint.

Antony Turner

A kilogram (2.2 pounds) of CO_2 would fit in a balloon like this 3 feet across.

1 kg CO_2

"'Carbon footprint' is the term for all the emissions of CO_2 that a person or a company is responsible for," Antony explains.

For people like you and me, that means adding up all the emissions from the electricity we use, the food we eat, and the miles we travel. There are lots of websites that help individuals and families calculate their carbon footprint. But for whole companies, with hundreds or thousands of factories, offices, vehicles, or shops, it's much more complicated. Antony's team of experts looks at every bit of what a business does and adds up the emissions from every part—from making things to advertising them and transporting them to stores;

everything, in fact, from the machines in the factory to the fluffy carpet in the director's office!

"We look at the total carbon footprint of any product or service."

That might mean the footprint made by the supplying of several million people with phone and Internet services, or the footprint made by the manufacture of a bag of chips.

Antony's job doesn't end with producing a list of figures:

"The numbers alone are not enough," Antony says, so CarbonSense uses all sorts of techniques, such as specially created graphics and animations, to help people to visualize the greenhouse-gas emissions of their business and make climate change real for them.

CarbonSense has worked with all sorts of businesses, from TNT—which delivers letters and parcels in two hundred countries—to the Honda racing-car team. And every time, really seeing their carbon footprint and understanding what it means makes a difference: companies shift to energy-saving ways of working and start to think seriously about how they can cut their emissions to almost nothing in the future.

"If we reach their hearts," Antony says, "they may decide to do something really creative, really out of the box. That's what we hope for."

Of course, it isn't just big business that needs to visualize its carbon footprint; we ALL need to do it:

"Every person, organization, community, and country needs to know the basic carbon math: how much they are responsible for and what parts of their lives are the highest-emitting."

Antony calls this being "carbon literate."

"The most important task facing human society now is getting about one billion people carbon literate in the next five years," he says. "Human creativity needs to be unleashed for this most massive challenge."

Gaia Warriors

" There is still time to avoid the worst impacts of climate change, if we take strong action now. "

NICHOLAS STERN

(A top, top economist who has advised governments and banks in the U.K. and around the world. He's the author of the Stern Review, the U.K. government report published in 2006 about what climate change is going to cost the world.)

SO, HERE'S THE PROBLEM:

Our planet is warming up, and in your lifetime and that of your children, it's going to get a lot warmer.

The level of CO_2 in the atmosphere today is 380 ppm (that means parts per million; in other words, in every million parts of air, 380 of them are CO_2). Add in the other greenhouse gases, and that gives the same effect as 440 ppm of CO_2.

This amount of greenhouse gas in the atmosphere is likely to make the climate at least 3°F warmer than it is now, perhaps as much as 7°F warmer.

A planet 7°F warmer than the one we live in now would be a very different sort of place. **A planet no human has ever yet experienced.**

To improve our chances of survival, we need to slow the rate of climate change to give us more time to adapt, and keep the planet from warming up any more than is now inevitable.

That means cutting greenhouse-gas emissions drastically as soon—as close to NOW—as we can, to keep levels from going above 450 ppm and to start the long process of returning them to 350 ppm.

On a personal level, this means reducing your greenhouse-gas emissions from a column balanced on a picnic table to one balanced on the palm of your hand.

AND HERE IS THE SOLUTION?

STOP.

Just **stop.**

Turn out the lights, close down the power stations, leave the cars at the side of the road, shut down the factories, ground all the airplanes.

Our slogan could be "Back to the Stone Age"!

Simple, eh?

NO, HERE IS THE SOLUTION:

Trouble is, this "Back to the Stone Age" approach wouldn't work, even if everyone agreed to follow it, because we can't support 9 billion people (which is how many of us there'll be by 2050) on Stone Age farming and technology.

There are a lot of things we **will** have to stop doing, like driving everywhere, flying every time we go on vacation, eating whatever we want, and having lots of deep, hot baths. But then, most of the people in the world have never been able to do those things anyway, so it's only fair that we should stop being so greedy and selfish with the planet's resources.

So "stopping" is part of the solution—but we can't stop growing food, building homes, keeping them warm and light, and getting from place to place. At the moment, doing all those things depends on fossil fuels. Not only in the obvious ways, like cars running on gasoline and power stations burning coal or gas. The wheat in your breakfast cereal and the cotton in your jeans needed gas-powered machines to grow and harvest them, as well as planes and trucks to take them to the store you bought them from; the concrete used to build your house was made in a kiln heated by burning coal; and your iPod, your computer, and your phone were made from oil-based chemicals in factories powered by fossil fuels.

So we have to change how we do things, which means the solution isn't simple and it isn't just one thing. But it isn't just a dream, either. It's being built, right now, from lots of smaller solutions, by people all around the world—solutions that help us cut our greenhouse-gas emissions and solutions that help us prepare for the climate change we can't avoid.

This section of the book is about some of those solutions and the people who are working on them. Some are finding ways to fight climate change by trying to change how we live our everyday lives; others are fighting on a bigger scale, by trying to change what governments and countries do. Reading about them, you'll learn more about what a far-reaching problem climate change is—and also that there are as many ways of fighting it as there are people in the world.

Changing Minds

The biggest obstacle to beating climate change is inside people's heads. If you haven't gotten the message that climate change is real and we need to stop it, then you won't change the way you live or ask your government to help cut greenhouse-gas emissions. As the great scientist Albert Einstein said, "You cannot solve a problem with the same thinking that caused the problem."

Casper Ter Kuile and Emma Biermann are co-founders of the environmental network U.K. Youth Climate Coalition (U.K. YCC, ukycc.wordpress.com), which brings together youth organizations for a strong political voice on climate change. They want to make sure that the message gets to as many young people as possible.

"We are the generation who will have to live with climate change and pay for it," says Casper. **"So let's get fired up about it."**

But how do you get people who are pretty occupied with clubbing, drinking, and checking out their friends on Facebook to care about the planet?

Casper and Emma with a polar bear (look carefully!)

All photos: U.K. YCC

"You've got to bring climate change into people's world, get their heroes to lead them. If the coolest guy in class starts to care about climate change, then others will follow."

The way that climate change is often represented in the media is definitely not the way to do it:

"Telling someone the world is going to end and they are a bad person because they don't switch the lights off is not effective," says Casper. "It just doesn't work to make people feel guilty and powerless."

The message that U.K. YCC wants to convey is much more positive:

"The things we need to do to tackle this problem will actually give us all a much more enjoyable lifestyle," says Emma. "Yes," agrees Casper. "Fewer cars, locally grown food, cleaner energy, better public transport. We'll be healthier and happier and — oh, yeah — we'll be fighting climate change!"

From left: Emma; Lauren, from the Australian Youth Climate Coalition; and Casper

U.K. YCC encourages members to get active—to tell politicians, local councils, and school governors what needs to be done.

"We know there are lots of young people who care about the planet, quietly, at home in their rooms," says Emma. **"YCC will give them the little push they need to get them out of their bedrooms to take some action."**

As experienced campaigners, Casper and Emma know how powerful young people can be as a force for change, not just in their own homes and schools, but on the big political stage too. Casper says:

"A group of fourteen-year-olds making a well-informed appeal to their MP [Member of Parliament] can have much more effect than adults doing the same."

U.K. YCC representatives will be at all future rounds of international negotiations on climate change, along with other young climate campaigners from around the world, demanding that governments take action to safeguard their future.

© Greg Armfield/WWF-U.K.

Casper on the sofa with Minister for the Environment Hilary Benn

Check out
www.mygreenfinger.org
for more about the
Greenfinger campaign.

Young climate campaigners
from all over the world

"It's up to us to tell all the delegates that our generation will not accept failure," says Casper.

U.K. YCC has serious work to do, but having a good time is also an essential component of climate campaigning:

"The more campaigning I do," says Casper, "the more fun I have."

And if you don't believe him, take a look at the GreenFinger campaign" (see link above). I won't tell you any more about it, but it's a great way to have a laugh with your friends . . . oh, yeah, and deliver a very important message.

EMMA'S **TOP TIPS** FOR THE RELUCTANT CAMPAIGNER, OR "HOW TO GET OFF YOUR BED AND CHANGE THE WORLD"

Casper and Emma when they started the U.K. Youth Climate Coalition

BE A SPONGE: Read, watch, listen — soak up anything that makes you angry, passionate, and fired up for action.

DO WHAT YOU ARE GOOD AT: Whether that's art, theater, music, talking, listening, writing — your skills will make your campaigning AWESOME!

STEAL IDEAS: You don't always have to come up with your own ideas — it's fine to use someone else's.

REMEMBER — SMALL IS POWERFUL: Just as Anita Roddick said, "If you think you're too small to have an impact, try going to bed with a mosquito."

HAVE A GOOD TIME: You'll get through to people better if you work with friends and enjoy your campaigning.

ALWAYS CARRY CHOCOLATE CHIP COOKIES: Essential equipment for attracting instant support and boosting campaigner morale!

Richard Ford—Footprint Friends

FOOTPRINT FRIENDS

www.footprintfriends.com

This is a site exclusively for young people (aged eleven to eighteen) to air their views on climate change and enter competitions to win funds for eco-projects. Upload your "footprints"—paint your feet to symbolize the footprint you want to leave on the planet.

C-CHANGE

Young people educating other young people about climate change.

www.switchonswitchoff.org

STUDENTS ON ICE

www.studentsonice.com

Runs expeditions to the Arctic and Antarctic for young people

JULIE'S BICYCLE

Devoted to taking the heat out of music—reducing the carbon footprint of the music biz, including going to festivals.

www.juliesbicycle.com

OTHER WAYS OF CHANGING MINDS

ARTS vs. GLOBAL WARMING

CLIMATE CHANGE EDUCATION www.climatechangeeducation.org/art
A collection of resources — videos, music, visual arts, and more —
about fighting climate change.

CAPE FAREWELL www.capefarewell.com
Combines art, science, and education to communicate about climate
change in new ways. Leads expeditions to the Arctic with artists
and scientists and has led two expeditions with young people.
Check out expedition blogs, photos, and videos.

FORKBEARD FANTASY combines film, performance, and animation
in a whirl of mayhem. Its show *Invisible Bonfires* is a crazy comic
parody of climate-change lectures and conferences.

www.forkbeardfantasy.co.uk

THE 11TH HOUR is a documentary
movie about what we need to
do to save the planet, narrated
by Leonardo DiCaprio.

Forkbeard Fantasy

DEMONSTRATIONS

The Energy Action Coalition was founded in 2004, bringing together dozens of groups of young people around the country dedicated to clean energy. In 2007, 3,000 members descended on Capitol Hill to show Congress that young people care about the climate.

www.energyactioncoalition.org

BOOKS

Kate Evans's cartoon book Funny Weather will make you laugh out loud while you learn lots of stuff about climate change.

Former Vice president Al Gore has a version of his book, An Inconvenient Truth, adapted for younger readers.

Andy Hollingworth

Marcus Brigstocke

POSTERS

TO SAVE THE PLANET

good50x70.org/2009/gallery/climate-change

COMEDY

Comedian Marcus Brigstocke went to the Arctic with Cape Farewell to see the big melt for himself and bring back jokes. "The Arctic is melting faster than the Wicked Witch of the West in an outdoor bath with the shower on in the rain."

TECHNOLOGY

The World Summit Youth Award is given to an online project that addresses the U.N.'s Millennium Development Goals. Check out the winning projects in all categories, including Go Green! **www.youthaward.org**.

Bad Habits

Humans are good at habits, like always getting a ride to school, or always standing under the shower for half an hour, or always using a blow-dryer. But changing old, energy-guzzling habits and developing new CO_2-cutting ones is easier than it seems—especially if there's an immediate reward.

Neil Jennings was doing a PhD at the University of East Anglia in the U.K. when he started noticing that students in the residence halls were in the habit of leaving the lights on all night. There was no incentive for anyone to bother to turn them off, because students paid a flat rate for their rooms, with no separate bill for electricity.

Neil's thesis was about one of the possible disastrous consequences of climate change—the failure of the Gulf Stream:

Neil Jennings of STUDENT SWITCH OFF, an energy-saving

"If the Gulf Stream shut down now, we would have a climate similar to that of Iceland, with sea ice off the south coast and snow on the ground until March every year — it would basically completely mess up our transportation system and agriculture."

Neil Jennings

competition
between university
residence halls

Luckily, most climate models predict that this is pretty unlikely to happen—maybe a 5% chance in the next one hundred years. **"But,"** says Neil, **"would you stay on a plane that had a 5% chance of crashing?"**

It's not surprising that Neil's mind kept wandering to all that CO_2 being added to the atmosphere, increasing the risks of nasty climate-change-consequences, just because no one could get into the habit of turning off the lights.

So he came up with Student Switch Off (SSO)—an energy-saving competition between university residence halls; they would compete against one another to reduce their energy use, and the ones that did the best would get prizes.

"The uni were very keen as soon as I told them about the idea," says Neil, **"as long as I did all the work!"** And there was quite a lot of work to do. First, Neil had to sort out practical details, like electricity meters: for the competition to be workable, the electricity used by each residence hall had to be separately measured.

Next, Neil needed prizes good enough to make winning worthwhile.

Luckily he got off to a flying start: **"My first sponsor — Ben and Jerry's — said yes within three hours of my first e-mail! Once I had one on board, the others were more interested."**

Neil ended up with five different companies sponsoring the scheme, providing prizes from free ice cream to movie tickets and solar-powered iPod gizmos.

The scheme was launched in September 2006, and the students seemed to like the *idea*, but Neil didn't know if they would really take *action*.

"The first indication we had that it was a success was in November, when the meter readings came in for October and showed a big reduction in energy use."

In its first year at UEA, Student Switch Off reduced the residence halls' carbon emissions by 132 tons, or 11%. Not huge, but a really significant start, and one that the university liked a lot, because it saved them money. It also got Neil selected by Ben and Jerry's as a "Climate Change Ambassador" to go to the Arctic with the World Wildlife Fund to see the impact of global warming firsthand.

"I was already convinced about climate change, but it was still quite shocking to see the changes in the depth of the ice. We drilled cores through the ice showing it was 1.5 meters [5 feet] thick, where twenty years ago it had been 2.5 meters [8 feet]."

Neil's Arctic adventures inspired him to roll out SSO to even more universities. In 2007–2008, the seven SSO universities on board reduced energy usage by an average of 8.7% and saved a total of more than 500 tons of CO_2. Four more universities signed up for 2008–2009, and another twenty-two started in 2009–2010.

Odeon Cinemas, one of the sponsors of SSO, has been so impressed that they've started their own "switch off," turning off lights and air-conditioning in their theaters overnight, saving £15,000 (more than $20,000) on fuel bills in just six months and significantly reducing carbon emissions.

"I wouldn't call myself a deep green," Neil says; **"I'm very pragmatic. Whatever takes the most CO_2 out of the atmosphere is best."**

Check out
studentswitchoff.co.uk

LITTLE CHANGES — BIG EFFECT

GREEN LIVING HANDBOOK

www.empowermentinstitute.net/glh

This six-step program is all about practical changes that everyone can make. It encourages groups of people to work together and reduce their garbage, water use, and energy use — all by doing small, simple things.

FOOTPRINT FRIENDS' WIPE OUT WASTE (WOW) CAMPAIGN

WOW provides special monitors that measure just how much energy a home is using and how much it costs. It clarifies the link between what you do and the energy you use, helping to change

BAD ENERGY HABITS.

(There are lots of other WOW campaigns around the world, focused on other sorts of waste, like trash.)

LITTLE DEMONSTRATORS — BIG EFFECTS

In August 2008 a replica of a coal-fired power station at Legoland in Denmark was attacked by inch-high Lego demonstrators, who unveiled a banner saying "STOP CLIMATE CHANGE." Meanwhile, at the site of the real power station at Kingsnorth, hundreds of real humans demonstrated too.

World Development Movement/Peter Taylor

JUNEAU, ALASKA

THE CITY lost most of its power supply in early 2008 when a series of avalanches destroyed power lines. So citizens just turned off anything that wasn't really needed — half-empty freezers, TVs on standby, lights in hallways. In two weeks they'd cut their use of electricity by 30% — just by remembering to flick a switch or two.

Alaska Electric Light & Power Company

Keeping Turned On

Most of the electricity in the world at the moment is made by burning fossil fuels—like coal, oil, and gas. This means that every time you turn something on—a computer, a TV, a light—you're putting greenhouse gases (mostly CO_2) into the atmosphere, into your personal CO_2 column.

Of course, you can cut your CO_2 columns by using *less* electricity, but it's hard to use *no* electricity, unless you want to turn off every electrical appliance in your house and sit in the dark, without even a charged-up iPod to keep you company.

So we need new ways of making electricity—and concentrating solar power (CSP) could be one of them. Lawyer Polly Higgins was looking for ways to help the planet when she heard about it:

"I got such a buzz as soon as I heard about how CSP worked," she says. **"I knew at once that this was huge, important — a really big solution to the energy problem."**

In fact, Polly got such a buzz that she made spreading the word about CSP her new career, switching on politicians around Europe to the potential of this clean energy source. But what is CSP?

"I always ask people if they've ever burned their hand — or even

fried an ant — using the sun and a magnifying glass," Polly tells me. "Well, if you can fry an ant by focusing the sun through a little bit of glass, just imagine the power of hundreds and hundreds of huge mirrors all concentrating the sun's heat."

Ian Lawrie

Lawyer Polly Higgins

So CSP is very big-scale ant-frying—hundreds of mirrors reflect the sun's heat, concentrating it into a super-hot beam. That big heat is used to boil liquid, which drives turbines, changing heat energy into electricity.

"CSP isn't wacky new technology," Polly explains. "The first plants were built in America twenty-five years ago. So we know it works."

But how do you get electricity after sunset?

"CSP works using heat, and you can store heat in the day and use it to generate electricity after dark."

Of course CSP works best where it's very hot and very sunny—in a desert, in fact, and deserts are not something the world is short of.

"We'd need to cover just 0.3% of the area of the Sahara with CSP plants to generate all the electricity that Europe, the Middle East, and North Africa need."

But isn't it an awfully long way from the middle of the desert to where people live? Polly's got that one covered too:

"Some 90% of the world's population live within 2,700 kilometers [1,600 miles] of a desert," she says.

The idea is that high-voltage cables would carry the electricity into major cities, where it would plug into the existing grid and be transformed into the kind of electricity used in homes.

It all sounds so perfect that it's hard to understand why the desert isn't already covered in mirrors, supplying electricity from Marrakech to Moscow, Tel Aviv to Telford. The problem is that plugging new sources of energy like CSP into an old European electricity-grid system is almost impossible. Every country has its own grid—all are different and some very old-fashioned—and a whole lot of energy-generating companies want to keep control of the energy supply in order to make money. It's a terrible hurdle, and it could have blocked the development of new clean energy sources for decades.

Luckily, thanks to the hard work of people like Polly and her colleagues, the European Parliament in Brussels has realized that we really need these new sources of electricity very badly, so they have ordered that all the grids be modernized and that the companies cooperate so that the electricity systems of every European country are compatible with one another. The target is to complete this work by 2016 so that new, green sources of energy like CSP will be able to plug in anywhere and flow all over Europe. By 2020 many homes in Europe could be using electricity generated by a CSP plant in the Sahara! What's more, since the two things that many poorer countries have are sunshine and desert, CSP could one day supply clean, CO_2-free electricity to countries where turning on the lights has been a luxury few people could enjoy.

Polly is full of enthusiasm for the potential of CSP:

"It's so exciting to be working with something that's a big solution!" she says. But she's also a realist, and she knows that by 2050, with a world population of 9 billion, we'd need 10,000 CSP plants to supply just half the world's electricity if we continue using and wasting it the way we do now.

"Renewables are only part of the solution," says Polly. **"What we need is a seismic shift in humanity's attitude so we start to care for our planet."**

Wind, solar, **wave,** and HYDRO are renewable sources of energy, so called because unlike coal, oil, gas, and the uranium that's needed for nuclear power, they don't run out. They create energy without burning anything—so they produce no CO_2.

Some countries already get some of their power from renewables. Germany, for example, gets 15% of its electricity from conventional solar power—produced by the sort of solar panels you can have on your roof, which generate electricity or hot water. Many people in the U.K. now have solar panels on their roofs heating water for baths, showers, and laundry. China is keen on this technology, too, and plans to triple its use of solar-heated water in the next few years.

The European Parliament has pledged "20, 20, 20 by 2020"—a 20% cut in emissions, and 20% increases in fuel efficiency and the use of renewables. The U.S. government hasn't yet passed any legislation mandating renewable energy levels, but some bills are in the works.

RENEWABLE DRAWBACKS

The problem with renewables is that they don't supply energy all the time the way fossil-fuel generation or nuclear power does, so the energy they provide needs to be stored for nighttime or calm days. At the moment, the technology for storing electricity doesn't work very well—but people are trying to find ways to improve it all the time.

One way to help with the stop/start nature of electricity generated from renewables is to get power from a mixture of different sources, so the chances are that at least one of them will be working at any given time . . . although when everyone turns on the TV to watch *American Idol,* there could be problems.

There are concerns about the effect that wave farms and wind turbines will have on wildlife and on the natural beauty of wild places. Also, wind turbines sometimes use up land that we may need for growing food in the future. So we need to think very carefully about where we put our new, clean energy-making equipment.

OFF THE GRID?

All those power lines that traverse the United States are part of three large power grids that keep everyone supplied. The trouble is that parts of these grids are very old—the average power-generation station was built in the 1960s—and the whole thing is a bit old-fashioned. To make the most of renewables, we need a modernized grid and, perhaps, lots of smaller circuits, supplying communities with energy generated close to where people live and work. We could also use new combined heat and power (CHP) central heating boilers in people's houses and offices to generate electricity as well as heat; these should be available in the next five years.

Dale Vince, high-profile eco-warrior and head of Ecotricity, a renewable-energy company, says we can help now by choosing who we get our power from: "You can fight climate change with your electricity bill. Use your need for electricity to bring about new clean sources of it—sustainable ones."

GO NUCLEAR

One simple solution would be to replace our coal- and oil-fired power stations with nuclear power stations. These don't burn fossil fuels, and we'd need only a few of them to meet our needs. Currently, the U.S. gets about 20% of its electricity from nuclear power. But over their lifetime, nuclear power stations have a big carbon footprint—the uranium they run on has to be mined and transported, and the very long-lived toxic waste they generate has to be disposed of. Some people (for example, James Lovelock) think that this isn't a big problem and that we must "go nuclear" to combat climate change and keep the lights on. Other people (like me) would rather live with some power cuts to avoid nuclear.

A nuclear power station in Pennsylvania

CARBON CAPTURE

China and India can't switch to renewables quickly enough to power their fast-growing industries and cities. So they (and other countries with big coal reserves) are going to be using coal-fired electricity power stations for many years to come. To keep from pouring CO_2 into the atmosphere, we need carbon capture—this is the technology that catches CO_2 and stores it safely, usually underground. But the technology to make carbon capture work won't be ready until 2030 at the earliest, so countries that can manage without coal-fired power stations should do so until carbon capture is working perfectly.

Sir Robert Watson, Chief Scientific Adviser to the U.K. government, says, **"If there's one technology the world has to have, it's carbon capture."**

For MORE on our energy options

Check out the U.S. Department of Energy site dedicated to saving energy at:

www.energysavers.gov

It includes lots of information, including a whole section devoted to renewable energy at:

www.energysavers.gov/renewable_energy

They even have a great blog full of inspirational success stories, clear explanations of complicated topics, and energy efficiency tips.

www.eereblogs.energy.gov/energysavers

Driving Mad

Cars that run on gasoline produce a lot of CO_2—more than 10,000 pounds per car every year. When you add all the fossil fuels that get burned to make the car in the first place, the greenhouse-gas cloud above each car is even bigger. And there are about 250 million of them in the U.S. alone.

Almost half of all car trips are so short that most people could easily walk or cycle instead, and some of the shortest of all regular daily car trips are made by parents taking their children to school.

The solution here is pretty obvious, isn't it? Just get on your bike—and it's Holly Bruford's job to help school students in London to do just that.

"I have the best job in the whole of London," says Holly. **"I get paid to ride around on my bike every day!"**

Holly Bruford works for Sustrans (www.sustrans.org.uk), a U.K. charity that encourages planet-friendly, healthy ways of traveling. She helps run a project called Bike It in schools across London.

Bike It aims to get children biking to school instead of getting a ride in a car.

Each school-run car trip produces, on average,

Holly Bruford, Bike It officer

about two pounds of CO_2. With hundreds of thousands of children traveling to school by car, that's a lot of CO_2 that could be saved by "biking it." Holly's job is to show children and schools that biking to school is safe, fun, healthy, and good for the environment.

"As a field officer, I make my own schedule," she says. **"I might be running cycling-skills workshops for a bunch of children at a school, or talking to the staff about CO_2 emissions. I could be sorting out how to get a cycle shed built or organizing a bike festival to get people enthusiastic about biking."**

Holly's commitment to doing something practical to combat climate change began when she was working for an aid organization in Guatemala:

"In Britain the signs of global warming are still quite small, but in Guatemala they're huge. It's already changing people's lives and making them much harder. Winters there have become so wet that it's impossible for poor farmers to get their produce to market. So they have no income unless they can find a way to store their crops until spring. In a community on the poverty line, that creates real hardship."

Just before Holly left Guatemala in 2005, a fierce tropical storm caused catastrophic mudslides across the mountain region where she worked. The next-door village was simply wiped out:

"It was just a mass grave. Everyone was killed, because of climate change — caused by things happening in a world those people didn't even known about . . . our world, my world, back home."

When Holly returned to Britain, she was determined to make a difference:

"One of the best things about this job is that I'm working with people with the same morals, and with energy to put into something they really care about. And the kids are great fun!"

Holly and her colleagues at Sustrans are starting to have a real effect. Since the start of the Bike It project, four times more children from the schools taking part are regularly biking to school, and every year there are more and more schools that want to get involved. But convincing students and schools that biking it is a good idea isn't always easy:

"People often think it'll take ages. One little girl I met got to school at half-past seven because she'd allowed herself two hours to cycle a couple of miles!"

There are real practical problems to be overcome too, but these are just what Bike It was set up to overcome:

"Sometimes," says Holly, "I feel like a fairy godmother. Teachers say, 'Oh, but we haven't got a bike shed,' and I say, 'Here's a bike shed!' Kids say, 'But we haven't got any lights,' and I say, 'Here are your lights!' I'm the 'yes' girl. I'm the girl who says, 'I'll fix that; I'll make that happen.'"

Holly Bruford/Sustrans

"I feel like a fairy godmother"

Holly Bruford/Sustrans

PLANET-LOVING WAYS OF GETTING AROUND

A

Bikes and **feet** are the best options — but you can't bike to see your grandma 200 miles away, or walk 20 miles to the mall. So the next best option is the **bus** or the **train.** That way you'll be adding nine times (bus) or seven times (train) less CO_2 to your greenhouse-gas column than you would have by going in the car.

Trucks

Almost all the stuff we buy is taken to stores in diesel-powered trucks. Putting it all on trains instead would release 90% (!!) less CO_2 than truck transport.

We could also move freight around on canal boats as some companies are already doing to save money on fuel.

Electric cars

Gas stations could sell electricity from renewable sources to charge up electric cars instead of selling gas. It's all possible, but the car companies are not eager to make the big switch yet, so it may take a few more years. Also, electric cars still take energy to produce, so whatever way you look at it, we're going to need to do a LOT less car-driving.

VERY BUSY ROAD

Biofuels

Grow a plant, and it soaks up CO_2. Make it into biodiesel or ethanol and run your car on it, and it releases that CO_2 again; overall, the atmosphere hasn't gained, or lost, CO_2: that's the bright idea of biofuels. But most biofuels are a very bad idea, because forests (which soak up masses of CO_2) and food crops (that people need to eat) are being destroyed to grow plants for making biofuel. You could feed a person for a whole year on the grain it takes to make enough biofuel to fill up one tank, of one car, once. The only "good" biofuel is the stuff that can be made from recycled cooking oil — make your French fries, then fuel your car!

for more about
bad biofuels:

www.nature.org/initiatives/

climatechange/features/

art23819.html

Plane Foolish

I wish I could tell you that planes don't emit any greenhouse gases, that they are as planet-friendly as a field of cute little daisies in the sun. Then we could go on crossing the Atlantic in four hours and going halfway around the world for a weekend.

But they *do* emit greenhouse gases. Lots and lots. In fact, planes are about as planet-friendly as the meteorite in the movie *Armageddon*. It's not that planes are especially inefficient: they produce about as much CO_2 per passenger per mile as a car with four people in it. The difference is that you don't drive from LA to London; your per person CO_2 emission for that return flight would be two and a half tons, about the same as six months' worth of car travel in an average family car. What's more, that CO_2, plus a cocktail of other greenhouse gases, is emitted high up, where the plane flies, exactly where those gases can do the most damage, causing nearly three times more greenhouse warming than emissions lower down.

So it's clear we *should* be doing much less flying. But what we *are* doing is more and more. By 2030, air travel will have tripled.

Luckily, more and more people are realizing that flying isn't very good for the planet and are trying to find other ways to get around. Justin Schlosberg set up a company called Noflights.com to help people do just that.

Noflights.com was devoted to making rail and ship transportation available and affordable to more people. Justin told me:

Noflights.com

"People on all our trips and itineraries were making a meaningful reduction in their CO_2 emissions."

By booking seats on trains, ferries, and cargo ships, Noflights.com got you anywhere in the world without a plane.

Hell Is for Heroes

Justin in his band

Justin knows about no-flight travel, because he spent six years schlepping around the planet on a tour bus as a singer with the band Hell Is for Heroes:

"Touring taught me that not flying isn't a compromise or a sacrifice," says Justin. **"It's lots of fun and a great experience. We told our customers that although without flights they may have time to go only half the distance, they would see twice as much of the world."**

Sadly, Noflights.com no longer exists, but Justin's company blazed a trail and showed travelers a different way to globe-trot. The good news is that even big travel companies are getting interested in making travel greener by cutting the waste and energy use of hotels and tour operators and using trains, buses, and boats where possible. ABTA (the Association of British Travel Agents) told me that there's a huge move toward making travel more sustainable.

Although right now people are still flying way too much, the future of travel isn't in the air, because there's no good way to make flying earth-friendly. Planes won't work on electricity, like cars, and the extra plants we'd need to grow to make the right sort of biofuels to run planes could take up as much space as the area of China, which wouldn't leave much room for food or forests. Because only a tiny percentage of the world's population can afford to fly anyway, this would seem unwise.

It's clear that "no flights" doesn't mean "no travel," but it does mean that if we want to travel a long way, it's going to take days—even weeks—not hours. We need to think differently about traveling: instead of the journey being something unpleasant that you endure to get where you're going, it could become as important as the destination. As Justin said:

"Your journey is part of your holiday."

LOOK — No Wings

Campaign Against Air Travel
PLANE STUPID

is a network of groups taking inventive direct action against airport expansion and aviation's climate impact.

"Bringing the aviation industry back down to earth!"

www.planestupid.com

Take the pledge to avoid flying for 12 months at www.lowflyzone.org and tell your tales of slow travel there.

Carbon Offsetting

You'll find a carbon-offset option on most websites where you can book flights. The idea is that you pay someone to plant trees, buy a bit of forest, or give some low-carbon technology to a developing country. This is supposed to soak up the CO_2 your flight emits, so you can fly guilt-free.

There are a lot of problems with this idea, not the least of which is that there isn't room in the world to plant enough trees to "offset" everyone's flights. Even if all of the Southern Hemisphere ran on solar power, we'd still fry if the rest of us went on burning fossil fuels. If we really want to slow climate change, we should be reducing air travel A LOT, cutting our emissions in every way we can, AND planting trees and helping other countries use low-carbon technology.

To find out how saving forests can REALLY help,

see **www.worldlandtrust-us.org** and **www.coolearth.org**.

THE MAN IN SEAT 61

www.seat61.com

Ex-railwayman Mark Smith began seat61.com as a hobby in 2001, and now it's a full-time job. The site provides free information on traveling by train or ship instead of flying.

LOW-CARBON ADVENTURERS

Ed Gillespie traveled around the world in 2006 without taking a single flight. He says, "In an age when any idiot can get on a plane and twang themselves to the other side of the planet, there is something uniquely satisfying about a long voyage by sea." Read his blog:

www.lowcarbontravel.com

Ryan Van Duzer, broadcaster, travel writer, and video film-maker, known as the "Out There Guy" in his native Colorado, proves that you can have great globe-trotting adventures with nothing more than a bike and a tent. "Bicycling is the ultimate way to travel and see the world. I get to hear, smell, touch, and feel every inch of my adventures."

www.duzertv.com

Your Own Adventures without Flights

You can cross oceans and continents by train and boat. High-speed trains can get you to your destination as fast as a plane, if you add in the time you spend lining up at the airport.

Ferryboats can do short sea crossings, but for crossing the ocean, you need a cargo ship. Their CO_2 emissions aren't low, but they are doing an essential job, and you can just piggyback as a passenger. But beware of cruise ships! They are so luxurious that they have a carbon footprint three times greater than a plane per person per mile and thirty times more than a train trip!

Rock-Star Food

Next time you go to the supermarket, just take a minute to read the labels on the food. If it says the "country of origin" is Peru, Guatemala, Kenya, Israel, New Zealand, Egypt, or somewhere equally far away, it's clear that your dinner is better traveled than you are. It has zoomed around the world like a rock star, burning up aviation fuel and loading the atmosphere with ever more CO_2. And all of that's before you add in the emissions from the tractors, fertilizers, and pesticides it took to grow the food in the first place. Even supermarket foods that aren't flown in from other countries do an absurd amount of traveling, from farms to packaging plants, to warehouses, to grocery stores.

And the energy craziness doesn't stop when the food arrives at the supermarket: it's displayed in chilled cabinets with no doors, next to heaters and bright lights; then people drive their cars to buy it and take it home. If you wanted to design a way of feeding people that wasted the most energy and created the greatest greenhouse-gas emissions possible, this would probably be it.

Duncan Gibson, former chief executive officer of the organic-food delivery service Abel & Cole in the U.K., isn't impressed:

Duncan Gibson, former CEO of Abel & Cole, which promotes food with a low-carbon footprint

www.abelandcole.co.uk

"If you showed a freshly landed Martian the way we produce and sell food, they'd think it was utterly ridiculous," he says.

So how did it get this bad?

"For the last thirty years," Duncan explains, **"supermarkets have been working out how to sell a lot of food and to sell it very cheaply. So they grow food on a huge scale, and everything is centralized."**

That means fewer, bigger farms, and food traveling long distances.

For example, a major U.K. supermarket is about to build a big meat-processing and packaging plant in Uruguay, to supply U.K. stores. (Yes, that's Uruguay in South America, and the U.K. in Europe.)

Duncan comes from a farming family and could see what supermarket-style food was doing to farmers, food, and the planet. So he tried to change the supermarkets from the inside, running the fresh-produce side of several major U.K. companies. But he soon realized he wasn't going to be successful, so he moved to Abel & Cole, which was already supplying organic food that hadn't been on a world tour before arriving on the table:

"About 75% of all the food we supply to our customers is grown in the U.K. We do buy in some things from other countries — such as bananas and wine — but we never use air freight. It all comes on boats."

Abel & Cole doesn't package things the way supermarkets do, either.

Almost everything comes in simple cardboard boxes, which customers return, so they can be reused and then recycled when they finally wear out. Everything they sell is organically grown, which cuts down on emissions from chemical fertilizers and pesticides, and finally it's delivered to its customers, so there's no need for energy-wasting freezer units and overlit, overheated stores.

"Each of our vans delivers to eighty or ninety homes," says Duncan. **"So that's eighty or ninety cars that aren't driving to the supermarket a couple of times a week. But,"** he adds, **"we do have trouble with our fuel. We've tried using recycled chip fat [see "Planet-Loving Ways of Getting Around," page 116], but our vans stop and start so much, their engines keep blowing up! I'd really love to find a way to sort that out."**

More and more people are shifting away from supermarket food, so companies like Abel & Cole are growing, and working with more and more farmers, bakers, and cheese makers to

Abel & Cole

*Please look after our box, keep it dry, and leave it out for us. You never know... you might see it again someday.

supply people with food that comes from near where they live. But sometimes food-miles are unavoidable:

"Certain foods grow best in certain areas," Duncan explains. **"We try to use local soils and climate sympathetically, but that means you have to move stuff around."**

Apples, for instance, don't grow so well in the north of England, so Abel & Cole is encouraging farmers in Kent, in the far southeast corner, to replant apple orchards that were pulled up because U.K. supermarkets started buying their apples from abroad. Duncan's apples will have to travel, but not on a plane from the other side of the world.

Locally produced food is often cheaper than the imported alternative, but organic foods are generally more expensive, because organic farming can't produce such high yields. Duncan hopes that even in a recession, when people have to cut back on their spending, customers will stick to their decision to buy more planet-friendly food:

"The last thing we should do is pile back into producing food that uses more and more oil. In the long term, fuel prices and the environmental costs will mean most food will be produced and delivered our way."

YUM, YUM, YUM! SNACK WITH A LITTLE FOOTPRINT

Tips on what to eat...

* EAT FOODS IN SEASON. Fresh strawberries in January come from a LONG way away (unless you live in Australia) or were grown in heated greenhouses.

* EAT LESS MEAT AND DAIRY. A kilogram (2.2 pounds) of beef is responsible for more greenhouse-gas emissions than three hours' driving AND leaving all the lights on back home. Farm animals produce lots of methane and eat food that could feed humans.

* DRINK TAP WATER. Bottled water is transported a long way, the plastic bottles take energy to make, and most get thrown away. The bottled-water industry causes 2.5 million tons of CO_2 emissions a year.

and where to buy food...

* BUY LOCAL. Use farmers' markets (which mostly sell stuff that's produced within 30 miles) or farm share programs (which deliver a box of vegetables and fruit, often organic and mostly local) whenever you can. If you have to choose between something grown locally and in season and something grown organically in another country, choose local.

Look online for Community Supported Agriculture to find out more.

✱ IN THE SUPERMARKET... Read the labels and buy food produced in your country or state. Ask the supermarket manager to stock locally grown food.

Grow your own

✱ YOU CAN GROW SOME FOOD—even if it's only a pot of herbs and all you have is a windowsill. There are tons of books, websites, and magazines that will tell you how to get started.

✱ ENCOURAGE YOUR SCHOOL TO START A VEGETABLE GARDEN. For information on how to get started, visit

www.kidsgardening.org.

✱ HOME-GROWN FUTURE. The droughts, floods, and extra-hot summers that climate change is going to bring are going to have a big effect on how much food we can grow and where. Some countries may no longer be able to grow enough food to sell to other nations, so it's important that we try to grow as much food close to home as we can.

Homes for Climate Heroes

Most buildings are as leaky as a sieve. When the weather's cold, the heat leaks out, and when it's hot, it leaks right back in again. To keep the temperature inside comfortable, we have to use central heating and air-conditioning a lot of the time. Architect Jim Logan knows that this is more than crazy and expensive; it's quite simply costing the earth.

"Every dollar you spend on your power bill," he says, **"impacts not only on your finances but on the future of the planet."**

And the impact buildings have doesn't stop there. There's all the embodied energy too—that's the power used to build them (to make the concrete, the steel, the bricks, and the glass) to transport all these, and to put them all together.

"Buildings in the U.S. are responsible for 35% of the country's carbon emissions, and it's growing," says Jim. **"As architects, we have great potential to reverse this trend. We need to invest talent and money now toward the evolution of an architecture that does not destroy us."**

Reversing that trend is what Jim Logan has been doing for more than thirty years. He designs buildings that don't have such a big impact on the planet. He has perfected the techniques of green design, using super-insulated walls and roofs; double- or triple-glazed windows with special high-tech coatings, oriented to catch heat when it's needed and be shaded when it's not; and skylights to make the best use of natural light. The buildings Jim designs are not leaky at all; in fact they leak so little that they don't need any source of heating or cooling and stay a steady 70°F or so winter and summer, even when the outside temperature drops to 20°F or soars to 100°F. Wherever possible, they are made with locally sourced materials that are easy to maintain and will last, which all helps to keep embodied energy low.

Why aren't all buildings like this?

"It's cheaper to build things badly than to build them well," says Jim. **"And the average American moves every three years, so if you tell them insulation will pay for itself in five years, they say, 'I won't be here.'"**

But things are changing. Sweden and Norway don't allow badly built houses—by law, their houses must be properly insulated, so they use just a quarter of the energy for heating that U.S. and U.K. houses do. In his hometown of Boulder,

Michael Shopenn

Eco-architect Jim Logan

Colorado, Jim has lobbied for laws that will require all new building designs to be computer tested for energy efficiency; anything that fails can't be built.

"Builders are very resistant to these changes," says Jim. **"But public opinion in Boulder is so pro-eco-build that their opposition has been swept away. They don't even turn up to meetings to oppose decisions anymore."**

Jim knows that not everyone can live in a new house, so his latest and biggest idea is the Boulder Energy Project:

"It's simple, but giant," Jim says. **"We're going to look at all the residential buildings in our town and look at their CO_2**

emissions — all 330,000 metric tonnes [360,000 tons] of them — and figure out a cost-effective way to fix them and try to make them all carbon neutral by 2030."

Jim and his team will use every green building trick they know to plug the energy leaks of Boulder's buildings—from the latest in solar power and insulation to putting a fan in the front door to track down drafty holes and then blocking them up with spray foam!

"We're trying to show that it's possible. It's a giant research project, really, and it's generating quite a buzz," says Jim. **"Every architect wants to say they're green now."**

GREEN-HOUSE LIVING

GOOD IDEAS:

Design makes a difference

The emissions from whole cities can be shrunk if they're designed and planned so that people don't have to drive everywhere and can walk or cycle wherever they need to go.

"If we have giant cities all over the world, with big highways for big cars, the world is not going to be a sustainable place." Enrique Penalosa, former mayor of Bogotá, Colombia

City trees cast cooling shade and provide shelter from cold winds — reducing the need for air-conditioning and heating. And they soak up CO_2!

Architecture to green the desert

Climate change will reduce rainfall and create deserts in many areas, so architects Michael Pawlyn and Charlie Paton have come up with the Sahara Forest Project. They've created greenhouses that produce their own fresh water from seawater using solar power. This will allow almost any food crop to be grown in the middle of even the hottest desert.

CONCRETE PROBLEMS:

To make concrete, you need to heat crushed rock to 2,730°F (1,500°C), so it isn't surprising that all the concrete we use is responsible for 5% of the world's CO_2 emissions. But a new kind of concrete that can be made at just 1,200°F (650°C) is being developed. Not only does it use less fuel to make, it actually soaks up CO_2 when it hardens.

GOOD STUFF TO DO AT HOME:

✓ Track down drafts and block them up.

✓ Check your attic insulation. . . . You need at least ten inches.

✓ Use windows, not air-conditioning, for cooling.

✓ Draw curtains as soon as it gets dark to stop heat leaks.

LEARN MORE

.Visit **www.ecofriendlyhouses.net to find out all about making a home earth-friendly.**

For more advice, check out www.GreenDIY.ie.

Maxwell's Photography

This website is put together by student Cara Augustenborg to help people make their homes climate-friendly. Cara also put together a little model house at a Dublin shopping center to show people all the things they can do to shrink their home's carbon footprint.

Cara, center, gets ready for some Green DIY.

Dressing for the Climate

I have to start this section with a confession: I am a clothes addict. My T-shirts alone fill two drawers, my double closet bulges, and I'm too embarrassed to tell you how many pairs of shoes I have. Every single item of clothing that I own has its own big, fat footprint, its own little column of CO_2 and trail of polluting chemicals. The cotton in my jeans and T-shirts was grown using pesticides that take a lot of energy to make, and then pollute land and water when they're used. I try to buy things made of organic cotton now, but that isn't exactly innocent either—it takes just as many gas-powered farm vehicles to cultivate and harvest organic cotton, and it gets transported to its final destination on a plane or a huge ship, just like the non-organic stuff. My favorite black pants are made from polyester, a kind of plastic derived from oil, and my favorite purple sweater is made of wool from New Zealand.

I'm not the only one with this planet-bashing addiction to new clothes: the average U.S. household spends more than $1,500 a year on clothes and shoes. It's clear our clothes habit is costing the planet way too much—but fashion designer Nin Castle could be our salvation:

Nin Castle in her studio

"The fashion industry is sooo negative!" she says. **"The whole thing — from the way cotton's produced to how it's harvested and made into clothes. I set up my company, Goodone, to try to do something about all that."**

Nin's plan was to design clothes that made people feel good but didn't have a horrible environmental impact. She began by using organic cotton:

"But it was too expensive, and I didn't have any money," Nin says, laughing. **"So I tried using recycled clothes. I found I could make pattern pieces that would fit onto an old T-shirt or a jersey. I thought, 'Hey, this is just fabric!'"**

Nin had to mix and match material from several different old T-shirts or sweatshirts to make up one of her designs. But this meant she could incorporate bold contrasts of colors and shapes. The clothes were a big hit, and Nin's business was born:

"My labor costs are high, but my fabrics cost virtually nothing."

Nin is making use of some of the 1 million tons of clothing and fabric that end up in landfill sites in the U.K. every year. She and her team sort through 200 tons of old clothes every week, looking for stuff that they can reuse. This simple operation of making new clothes out of old can have a big impact: clothes made in this way have around half the carbon footprint of clothes made from new textiles.

Goodone is still a small company, but Nin wants to have a big effect:

"I want to be on the high street, where I can have the biggest impact and make the biggest change," she says.

So her next step will be to work with big sports-clothing brands, using up their faulty stock and ends of lines, to make her own new designer clothes.

Jess Bonham

Danny Rud

"I want to show the big companies how easy it is to do this. Every high-street shop should have clothes made of recycled fabric."

Nin still loves fashion, even though she wants to change the way it works:

"You've got to be in it to win it," she says. **"A lot of ethical design is a bit tame. I don't want to be pious or worthy, I just want to design beautiful, sexy clothes."**

Nin's "mix and match" style!

NIN'S TIPS FOR CLOTHES ADDICTS

BREAK THE FAST-FASHION HABIT

"Buy ONE thing that you really love and that's really well made, instead of three things that won't last."

2. USE A NEEDLE!

"Learn some basic sewing so you can extend the life of your clothes. My favorite jeans started life as wide-legged; now they're narrow-legged, high-waisted trousers."

3. BUY THE GOOD STUFF WHENEVER YOU CAN

"Make SOME of the clothes you buy organic, ethical, and recycled, even if ALL of them can't be that way. It'll help businesses like Goodone to grow."

4. SPEAK UP

"If you don't like what a retailer does — using child labor or non-organic cotton or whatever — write and tell them. You are the customer, and they need you."

1. Washing away the planet

Washing a load of clothes in cold water instead of hot saves about two pounds of CO_2, and usually gets clothes just as clean.

2. Planet color

White clothes get dirty more quickly and need more washing to get them clean. Wear colors and patterns that don't show the dirt.

3. Overalls and aprons are planet-friendly

Washing machines, tumble dryers, and irons use electricity and generate CO_2, so the less you wash your clothes, the better. This doesn't mean you have to go around with egg stains on your shirt . . . use aprons, overalls, and napkins whenever you're doing something messy.

4. Clothes care

Clothes last longer when they are put away (no, this is not just a nasty rumor spread by parents who want you to clean your room). Also, do not put your clothes in the laundry basket just because you can't be bothered to put them in a bureau or closet.

5. Swishing

A swishing party simply means one where you swap clothes. Everyone brings along at least one nice piece of clothing they don't want anymore. Then everyone swaps — and goes home with a new wardrobe! You can organize your own swishing party.

Keeping Gaia Green

These green areas of tropical forest are one of Gaia's most important temperature regulators.

One of the most important parts of Gaia's temperature-regulation system is the green band of tropical forests around the earth's middle. It soaks up CO_2 and releases life-giving oxygen as trees grow, and it breathes out water vapor—making clouds and rain, which cool the hot, sun-soaked tropics. And of course it holds on to a lot of CO_2, keeping it locked up in the chemicals that make roots, trunks, leaves, and branches.

It doesn't take a genius to see that, in our current climate crisis, tropical forests could be a big, big help, and we *should* be protecting every single tree.

Roberto Pedraza

" I support the notion that tropical forests and other critically threatened habitats and their wildlife must be saved at all cost. "

SIR DAVID ATTENBOROUGH

(Sir David is a natural-history expert, wildlife filmmaker, and author. Several generations of people have been turned on to wildlife through his programs. He is my TOTAL hero.)

Roberto Pedraza

What we ARE doing is cutting trees down as if our lives depended on it. Around fifty soccer fields' worth are cleared every hour for timber, or to make room for farming, or, craziest of all, to grow biofuels for cars. This deforestation releases the CO_2 stored in the trees, it keeps those trees from soaking up more CO_2, and it releases another powerful greenhouse gas, nitrous oxide, from the exposed soil. Deforestation creates more greenhouse-gas emissions than all the cars, planes, and ships in the world. One-fifth of all the CO_2 released each year comes from deforestation. Not only that, but it plugs into a feedback loop—fewer trees means less rain, and less rain means fewer trees.

While governments argue about how to safeguard tropical forests, hard-working individuals all over the world are out in the woods, trying to save trees. Roberto Pedraza is one of them.

Roberto lives in the Sierra Gorda, a beautiful mountainous area of Mexico.

Roberto lives in the Sierra Gorda, a beautiful mountainous area of Mexico about the size of Rhode Island with many different kinds of natural tropical forests. Roberto works for Grupo Ecológico Sierra Gorda (GESG), a conservation organization founded by his parents:

"They were deeply concerned by the loss of the forests," Roberto explains. **"People were cutting down trees for fuel, for timber, and to make space for farming."**

The loss of the forests was starting to make life harder for the residents of the Sierra Gorda: without trees to soak up rain, and roots holding the earth, soil began to wash away, and floods and landslides were a problem.

"My parents began to work with their neighbors, educating them and planting trees."

A deforested slope before soil-conservation works began. Before slopes can be replanted, walls are built to hold soil in place.

All Roberto Pedraza

Roberto's parents' hard work paid off: the Sierra Gorda is now a reserve protected by the Mexican government and receives money from conservation organizations across the world. But local people are still the cornerstone of its success:

"Local people are our biggest allies," says Roberto. **"Around 34,000 participate each year in tree-planting, firefighting, and conservation activities."**

Roberto works with local landowners to encourage them to keep existing forests and to plant new native trees where forest has been cleared. The benefits for Sierra residents have been huge—water supplies are safer,

Ancient trees like those in the Sierra Gorda forest lock away many tons of CO_2 in their trunks, roots, and branches.

soil erosion has been cut, and there are more local jobs in forestry and ecotourism.

"After nineteen years," says Roberto, **"they are convinced of the benefits of conservation."**

Through protecting their forests, Roberto and the people of the Sierra Gorda are helping the whole world fight climate change now and in the future: now, by not cutting down fully grown forests and so keeping CO_2 safely locked up in trees; and in the future, by planting trees that will soak up lots of CO_2 when they get big in twenty years' time.

"We made an inventory of the carbon stored in our ecosytems and found that 124,065,851 metric tonnes [more than 136 million tons] of carbon is stored in the forests of the Sierra Gorda! So by protecting them, we avoid all that carbon being put into the atmosphere."

There are lots of reptiles and amphibians in Roberto's forests, like this baby salamander.

The forests of the Sierra Gorda are a lot more than a "carbon store." They hold 327 different species of birds, 131 species of mammals, and an astonishing 2,300 species of plants. As climate change could make 30% of the species alive today extinct, the Sierra Gorda is fighting not only the causes of climate change but the EFFECTS too, by keeping its species safe.

"Carbon is a great tool for conservation. We have returned 13,000 hectares [32,000 acres] of deforested land back to forest, and reduced fragmentation of forests," says Roberto. **"This means more and better habitats for wildlife."**

The Sierra Gorda's rich store of carbon and species means companies in the U.S. and Europe are keen to pay GESG to preserve their forests—and keep CO_2 locked up—to "offset" their own CO_2 emissions. Some climate-change campaigners are dead set against carbon offsetting (see "Plane Foolish," page 118), and it's true that if businesses and countries see it as an excuse not to cut their CO_2 emissions, it won't help at all in the long run. But if companies pay to save forests AND cut emissions, it could be a powerful way to lock up CO_2 and save species from extinction.

Right now, companies and individuals buying carbon offsets are helping to pay for GESG's work, allowing Roberto to safeguard more and more forest.

"Without our forests, we are doomed," he says. **"We need to protect what's left and recover what has been lost. Deforestation is not just CO_2 released, it means a loss of biodiversity; forests should be protected jewels."**

WOODLAND WAYS — Keeping Woods Woody

IN THE TROPICS

A big part of deforestation is driven by international business — logging, mining, and farming, especially for biofuels. The good part of this is that big international companies have to listen to public opinion — if their customers don't want them to cut down rain forests, then they have to stop.

CAMPAIGNING ORGANIZATIONS

Greenpeace

Well-respected, expert campaigners on every part of the environment. To find out how to help with rain forests:

www.greenpeace.org/international/campaigns/forests

The Rainforest Foundation

Check out their Tree-man blog. A man dressed as a tree travels around London to spread the word about forests and climate change:

www.rainforestfoundationuk.org/Tree-man

A barren slope before reforestation

WOODS AT HOME

Forests in the cooler parts of the world don't have such a huge role to play in the control of climate change, but they can still help to keep CO_2 locked up and protect biodiversity.

USEFUL ORGANIZATIONS

The Arbor Day Foundation

www.arborday.org

This organization inspires people to "plant, nurture, and celebrate trees."

BACKYARD WOODS

Plant a tree in your yard or somebody else's yard. Persuade your school to create a mini-woodland on the school grounds. Trees don't lock up much CO_2 when they are young, but in twenty years' time, when they are growing fast, they can lock CO_2 away in their woody trunks and branches. A single tree at maximum growth takes 15–30 pounds of CO_2 out of the atmosphere each year. Every little bit helps.

Roberto Pedraza

WOODS UNDER WATER

Sea Problems: Acidic and Warm

Billions of tiny floating sea plants — phytoplankton — lock away as much CO_2 as all the world's land plants. But climate change is making the seas warmer and more acidic, so phytoplankton may not grow as well and may soak up less CO_2, plugging us into another feedback loop — more global warming means less phytoplankton means more global warming.

Sea Problems: Coral Reefs

Coral reefs are often called the rain forests of the sea. They hold close to a million species of animals and plants. Corals like warm water, but if it's too warm, they die, and more acidic water makes it harder for corals to grow. So climate change could wipe out almost half of the world's reefs.

Liz Wood/Marine Conservation Society

Clown fish among
the tentacles
of an anemone

Green turtles, beautiful but threatened marine reptiles

Peter Richardson/Marine Conservation Society

Sea Solutions

Slowing climate change will help plankton and reefs, but we can take the pressure off them in other ways, such as by cutting pollution and preventing reefs from being used as building materials.

For More Sea Solutions

Check out the Marine Conservation Biology Institute website at

www.mcbi.org

66 **There is strong evidence of the rich countries causing the problem and poor countries being adversely affected, and thus it is time for the rich countries to address their obligations to reduce climate change.** 99

MARY ROBINSON

(Lawyer, ex-president of Ireland, and U.N. High Commissioner for Human Rights, 1997–2002 — and she's telling it like it is: "It's our fault, so we need to fix it.")

Martin Wagner and his son, Jasper

Martha Belcher

Lawyers for the Earth

If someone dumps garbage in your yard, they're breaking the law and they have to pay you for the damage they've done to your property. But no one owns the atmosphere, so when someone dumps greenhouse gases in it, how can they be made responsible for the damage that causes?

Lawyers like Martin Wagner of the environmental-law firm Earthjustice (whose motto is "Because the earth needs a good lawyer") are figuring out how this can be done.

Martin is using human-rights laws—some of the most important international laws there are—to help peoples like the Inuit to take action on climate change. Human-rights laws protect basic human needs, like a place to live, food, safety, and the culture that helps define who you are, and many people around the world are already losing their homes, their livelihoods, their safety, and their culture because of climate change.

"One of the strengths of the law," Martin says, **"is that it's a way to tell stories in places where they can make a difference. Human rights are about stories we can all relate to; stories about**

All photos taken by Martin Wagner

things we all need; powerful stories that can motivate powerful people to take action."

Back in 2001, Martin was one of the first lawyers to see the link between climate change and human rights:

"The Inuit were beginning to think about how to raise their plight with the world," Martin tells me, "at the same time as I was starting to think about using human rights to address climate change."

Martin sees the effects of climate change in the place closest to his heart, the Sierra Nevada mountains, where snowpack is decreasing and plant and animal species are threatened with extinction due to warming temperatures.

Martin began working with the Inuit Circumpolar Council on the effects that climate change was having on the lives of the Inuit. He and his colleagues interviewed Elders across Canada and in Alaska:

"It was remarkable to me how clearly they saw the effects of climate change on their environment,"

Martin says. He found that the Inuit had a detailed knowledge of seasonal changes, particularly relating to ice, that was passed down through generations and clearly showed how much the Arctic climate was changing.

"Ice is their highway, their grocery store, their shelter, even," says Martin, **"and all those things are being destroyed by global warming."**

It was clear to Martin that climate change was taking away the Inuit's human rights, and that the country with the biggest greenhouse-gas emissions—the United States—was clearly most responsible for that. So Martin and his team of lawyers helped the Inuit leaders and Elders present a petition to the Inter-American Commission on Human Rights in Washington, D.C. Martin said at the time:

"The United States makes up only 5% of the world's population but emits one-quarter of global-warming pollution. This petition calls on the United States to respect its human-rights obligations and take effective action to immediately reduce its contribution to the Inuit's injuries."

Before 2005, when the Inuit's petition was finally presented, talk of climate change was mostly technical and dry, but the petition changed all that. It made big news and helped people really understand the serious effects of climate change on humans.

"There is no international police force to enforce human-rights law," Martin explains, **"but discussing climate change in this way is**

very important because it influences decision-makers and nations and helps motivate ordinary people to take action."

The commission has not yet decided what to do about climate change and how it affects Inuit rights; but as a result of the Inuit's petition—and similar actions—the United Nations is now studying the link between global warming and human rights. Martin and his team have given the Office of the U.N. High Commissioner for Human Rights a legal document explaining how climate change violates people's rights and asking the U.N. to take action to help.

Martin is convinced that human-rights law is a powerful tool to use in the fight against climate change:

"Human rights crosses boundaries between liberals and conservatives. It puts governments under pressure by making them ashamed of what they've done wrong, but also making them aspire to do better!"

All over the world, people are starting to tell the stories of how climate change is affecting their lives through human-rights law, helped by lawyers like Martin:

"We are all in this struggle together," he says, **"and each of us is essential to making the world a better place."**

Rights AND Fights

RIGHTS AT RISK FROM CLIMATE CHANGE

TUVALU

Tuvalu is a tiny country just ten square miles spread over nine islands in the middle of the Pacific. In fifty to one hundred years it will be under the sea, and its 10,000 inhabitants will need some other country to give them a home. Tuvalu's neighbor, New Zealand, will accept only seventy-five Tuvaluan refugees per year, which would mean the last islander would reach safety long after Tuvalu had drowned.

At the moment, the U.N. doesn't recognize "country under water owing to climate change" as a good enough reason for someone to be an official refugee with a right to settle somewhere drier. But the Alliance of Small Island States, which represents other low-lying island countries such as the Maldives and Fiji, is working with lawyers to change things. (And to help publicize the fate of Tuvalu, Japanese photographer Shuuichi Endou is photographing every single one of Tuvalu's 10,000 people!)

CARTERET ISLANDS
Papua New Guinea

These tiny tropical islands will be under the sea even sooner than Tuvalu—by 2015, in fact. The islanders will have to go to the bigger island of Bougainville to live.

BANGLADESH

Bangladesh is the next country in line to have its human rights battered by climate change. Much of it is less than three feet above sea level, so a 16-inch rise in sea level could flood up to 94 million people, causing food shortages and outbreaks of waterborne diseases like cholera and dysentery.

FIGHTING WITH THE LAW

THE INUIT VILLAGE of Kivalina in Alaska is being washed away because of eroded sea ice, rising sea levels, and increasing storms. The whole community needs to move to another site, at a cost of some $400 million. So, with the help of lawyer Matt Pawa, Kivalina is suing ExxonMobil, eight other oil companies, fourteen power companies, and a coal company for causing the problem in the first place, and for conspiracy to mislead the public about the science of global warming.

GAIA'S RIGHTS

SUNDAY, SEPTEMBER 28, 2008, was a big day for Gaia — for the first time in history, it isn't only humans whose rights are protected by law. The people of Ecuador in South America have voted for a new constitution that recognizes that other species and wild places have the right to exist undisturbed and protects that right by law. This is the first big step toward the new and respectful attitude we all need to have toward our planet.

WINNING
WITH THE LAW

SIX GREENPEACE PROTESTERS tried to paint "Gordon Bin It" on the chimney of the proposed new coal-fired power station at Kingsnorth in Kent, England. They got as far as "Gordon" (referring to the prime minister of Britain) before having to stop, but still caused £35,000 (about $53,000) worth of damage. But when the case came to court in September 2008, the jury ruled that the protesters had a right to cause damage to the chimney to try to prevent the far greater damage that the coal-fired station would cause by contributing to climate change.

Hezel (4th from right) at the climate change conference in Bali

Baltz Tribunalo, Plan

Listening to Children

Hezel was just sixteen when she spoke to United Nations delegates and journalists from all over the world at the U.N. Climate Change Conference in Bali in December 2007. Hezel wrote in her blog at the time:

"I was not so nervous during the press conference. . . . At last I was able to tell everyone about the situation of children in our communities."

Hezel's community is a village on the island of Masbate in the Philippines. Hezel told the conference how, in her lifetime, climate change has caused the number of typhoons and storms to increase, bringing life-threatening flooding and landslides. She told them how, even when the immediate danger of the storm has passed, children are still affected: "There is failure of crops due to climate change," Hezel wrote in her blog, "and many children are not able to go to school because they have to work because their parents' income is not enough."

Children are much more vulnerable than adults to the disasters that climate change brings: being small makes them more easily overcome by water

FEMA/Leif Skoogfors

Baltz Tribunalo, Plan

Hezel fielding journalists' questions at the Bali climate conference, explaining why children's views about our environment are important

or mud; when crops fail because of flood or drought, they are the first to die of starvation; they are more easily killed by diseases such as cholera, dysentery, and malaria—all of which increase with climate change; and they suffer badly if they are separated from their families and have no one to care for them.

As children are the people worst affected by climate change, it's vital that they have a big say in what's being done about it. The organization Children in a Changing

Floods and typhoons destroy crops, businesses, and homes.

FEMA/Andrea Booher

Climate (CCC) is helping children's voices to be heard in their own communities and in the big wide world. CCC sponsored Hezel and other young delegates to attend the climate-change talks in Bali, and the organization works with children and young people across the globe.

"Children come up with ideas about how to solve problems," says Nick Hall of CCC. **"They have a longer perspective than adults and no prejudices."**

Nick Hall, environment enthusiast

Children are also particularly good at spotting the potential risks from climate-change disasters such as landslides and floods, because when they are outside playing they notice more than adults. Nick runs a program called Disaster Risk Reduction, which encourages children to make "risk maps" of their communities to show what the danger points are when disaster strikes:

"Children at a school in El Salvador spotted that a quarry on a riverbank was causing a risk of landslides and floods in their community," Nick tells me. **"They ran a campaign to get the mining stopped. They got their local government to stop the mining along their bit of the river and even over the border in Honduras."**

Campaigns like these change the way children are treated in their communities; grown-ups start listening, which makes children an important force for change. An elder in a village in Sierra Leone summed up what a lot of grown-ups feel: "We are amazed by the capacity of children to understand

and explain the range of risks and hazards faced by our community. They wake us all up to reality."

There are now many places in the world where children are helping their communities to prepare for the effects of climate change: planting trees to prevent landslides and provide flood barriers; teaching other children what to do when a typhoon strikes; reducing mosquito-carried diseases by clearing up stagnant water where mosquitoes breed; and of course speaking out and telling the world their stories, as Hezel did. Following his conversations with Hezel and the other young people, U.N. Secretary-General Ban Ki-moon told the climate-change negotiators in Bali:

"I've spoken to these young people, and it's your job to sort out their future!"

In the nine months following Hezel's return from Bali, the Philippines suffered three typhoons, one cyclone, and more floods and landslides.

" We want and have the right to be able to grow up in a sustainable and safe world. "

LEON, SIXTEEN

(Leon was a member of Plan U.K.'s Children's Advisory Panel when he said this. Plan U.K. helps children in poor communities around the world and listens to what children say.)

CHILDREN speaking out

Read Hezel's blog
and the blogs of other young delegates at Bali
and more recent U.N. climate-change talks:

childreninachangingclimate.blogspot.com

Nick and CCC will be helping more young people
speak on the world stage at future U.N. meetings
on climate change, working with organizations
that help kids get heard:

African Youth Initiative on Climate Change (AYICC)
"If students don't act against climate change, who will?"

Energy Action Coalition
U.S. campaigning organization started and run by young people
www.energyactioncoalition.org

YouthClimate.org
This site is a kind of "home base" for young people who are active in climate change.

NASTY numbers that will go UP with climate change

175 million
Number of children likely to be affected by disasters caused by climate change every year from now

3.5 million
Number of children who die every year from malnutrition

AND

800 thousand
Number of African children under age five who die every year from malaria

350.org
New youth-led global campaign to unite the world around a target atmospheric-greenhouse-gas concentration of 350 ppm CO_2. Includes a great animation at **www.350.org/mission**.

Peace Child International (PCI)
This international group empowers young people to "be the change they want to see in the world."

www.peacechild.org

Big Science

You only have to think of the different locations of a couple of human cities to see that human beings are good at coping with all sorts of climates. In Moscow you could get frostbite on a normal January day, but to cope with a chilly winter afternoon in Sydney, you'd need just a sweater. But if Sydney and Moscow suddenly swapped climates, there would be chaos. This is the big problem that climate change presents: unpredictability. How do you know when to plant your crops if the rainy season doesn't arrive at the time it used to?

This is where the work of the IPCC can help. The Intergovernmental Panel on Climate Change is a collaboration between more than 400 scientists from 120 countries. Its job is to use the best research into the Earth's climate to estimate how it will change in the next twenty to one hundred years, how this might affect people across the world, and what humanity can do about it.

Scientist Beth Holland

All four of the IPCC reports have been an important influence on what governments and the U.N. do about climate change. But the fourth report, published in 2007, was the most important:

"The evidence in the fourth report was more compelling, and more convincing," says Professor Beth Holland of the National Center for Atmospheric Research (NCAR) in the United States, one of the lead authors of the last two IPCC reports.

"When I did the distillation of all the scientific research, I was awed once again by the strength of the evidence."

The report woke up the whole world, and the world's governments, to the reality of human-made climate change.

But the job of the IPCC isn't simply to say, "Houston, we have a problem." Collaboration among scientists, and between scientists, economists, and politicians, is a key part of its work:

"It's really important," Beth tells me, **"that we translate scientific information into the impact it has on economics and on people's lives. We have to make sure that our transfer of scientific knowledge is as good as possible."**

One of the main tools that the IPCC uses to create a big picture of climate change worldwide, and its impacts, is computer modeling. But recently some things in the real world—such as the Arctic ice melt—have been happening faster than the IPCC models predicted. The models also struggle to reflect the seasonal changes in greenhouse gases caused by plant growth and decay. So for the next IPCC report, Beth and her colleagues need to add more detailed information about how climate works now to make the models better at predicting what will happen in the future.

"We're going back to first principles," says Beth, **"taking a more careful look at the ability of the earth's natural systems to soak up greenhouse gases, or release them and make matters worse."**

Beth, right, at Bridal Veil falls, Rocky Mountain National Park

Much of this huge "soaking up" depends on some of the planet's smallest inhabitants—microbes. This links to the early part of Beth's career, when reading about James Lovelock's Gaia had a big effect on her thinking:

"I realized that there was a bridge between the very small-scale activities of microbes in the soil and in the sea, and the composition of the atmosphere."

This link between the small and the big picture is what the IPCC is good at: linking scientific detail with consequences for millions of people. It's a link that helps to give us back that essential ingredient—predictability.

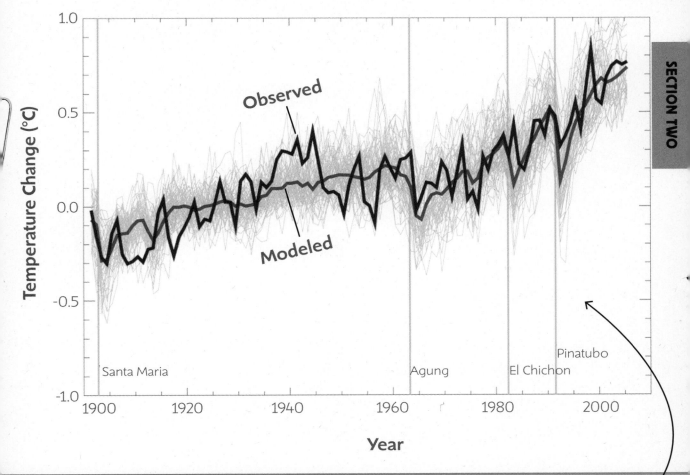

CLIMATE CHANGE WE **PREDICT** AND CLIMATE CHANGE WE **OBSERVE**

SECTION TWO

Observed

Modeled

Santa Maria   Agung   El Chichon   Pinatubo

Temperature Change (°C)

1.0

0.5

0.0

-0.5

-1.0

1900   1920   1940   1960   1980   2000

Year

After the IPCC graph in the Fourth Assessment Report of the 2007 study, FAQ 8.1 Figure 1.

This graph shows how the world's temperature REALLY changed between 1900 and 2000 and also how climate models SAY it changed. This is how climate models like the ones Beth works with are checked — by the opposite of forecasting, "backcasting," which means looking at temperatures that have already been measured.

A Short History of
TREATIES AND DEALS

1987: THE MONTREAL PROTOCOL

Scientists say, **"There's a serious hole in the ozone layer, and we need to fix it."** The U.N. listens, and the Montreal Protocol, an international agreement to cut emissions of hole-making gases, is signed. This leads to the formation of the IPCC.

1988: CREATION OF THE IPCC

1990: FIRST IPCC REPORT

The U.N. recognizes the need to talk about and act on climate change. From this time forward, information from the IPCC feeds into the world community and gradually starts to spur action.

1992: UNITED NATIONS EARTH SUMMIT IN RIO DE JANEIRO

Countries agree on the United Nations Framework Convention on Climate Change (trips off the tongue, doesn't it?). The UNFCCC doesn't set any targets for cuts in emissions, but it agrees that climate change is a problem and that the aim should be to stabilize climate. Not exactly big, but a start.

1995: SECOND IPCC REPORT AND U.N. MEETING IN BERLIN

This aims to give the UNFCCC some teeth. It is agreed that industrialized countries (which caused climate change in the first place) should be the first to make big cuts in emissions. The U.S. says it won't cut unless developing countries do too.

So there!

1997: KYOTO PROTOCOL U.N. MEETING IN KYOTO ON UNFCCC

This sets targets for cuts in emissions of 5.2% of 1990 levels for industrialized countries from 2008 to 2012. Pretty weak, but a start. The problem is not enough countries sign and ratify (that is, sign AND then say they'll stick to it) for it to become law.

2001: THIRD IPCC REPORT

This report makes even stronger statements about climate change and how humans are probably the cause of it.

2005: KYOTO PROTOCOL

The protocol is signed by enough countries to become law. The U.S. is still complaining about how difficult cutting emissions is for America, so it doesn't sign. Luckily the American people have more sense, and 600 mayors of U.S. cities have now pledged to keep their cities to Kyoto targets. California now pledges 80% emissions cuts by 2050.

But Kyoto is not completely toothless: it has set up ways in which developed countries can help poorer countries to preserve forests, put in new renewable energy sources, and change old polluting industries to cleaner, low-carbon ones. These projects are estimated to be keeping 2 billion tons of CO_2 out of the atmosphere.

2005, DECEMBER: BIG MEETING OF U.N. CLIMATE-CHANGE DIPLOMATS

The aim of this is to reach an agreement on what to do when Kyoto runs out in 2012. The U.S. negotiator walks out, and the only agreement other countries make is to talk about it all again.

2007: FOURTH IPCC REPORT

This report makes the boldest statement yet about climate change and makes headlines worldwide. There can be no doubt anymore: it's happening, and we have to do something about it.

2007: U.N. MEETING ON UNFCCC IN BALI

Serious wrangling takes place to try to agree on real action. The European Union pushes for 25%–40% cuts by 2020, but China, the U.S., and Japan say, "No way." An agreement to make "deep cuts" in emissions, but with no actual figures, is finally reached, but the U.S. says no—and then, at the last minute, says yes. So in the end there's an agreement with U.S. support, but a pretty weak one.

This was big. Representatives of 192 countries and 115 world leaders gathered in Copenhagen to try to reach an agreement on cutting greenhouse-gas emissions and fighting climate change. Thousands of climate-change campaigners—including some of the people in this book—came too, to see if they could influence the negotiations. Everyone came with high expectations, but the talks almost broke down. At the last minute the Copenhagen Accord was agreed on by some of the countries, including the U.S. and China, but it was not the strong commitment to action we'd hoped for.

Many people called the Copenhagen talks a complete failure. But at least all the countries agreed that climate change was real—even countries who'd been denying it before, such as Australia—and that we had to limit global temperature rises to 2°C (3.6°F). The Copenhagen Agreement will help cut emissions, set up a system to check on countries' emissions, and reduce deforestation. It's not perfect, but it's a start.

As I write this in May 2010, climate change negotiators are already working to prepare for the next big meeting in Mexico in November 2010. But it may take even more time, perhaps until the UNFCCC meeting in South Africa in 2011, for the world to agree to cuts in greenhouse-gas emissions that are set in law.

ALL TALK AND NO ACTION? Not quite: while governments wrangle with one another on the international stage, individual states and businesses are really coming to grips with the fact that "deep cuts" actually MEANS what it says. Remember California's example.

> "Whatever you can do, or dream you can, begin it. Boldness has genius, power, and magic in it. Begin it now."

JOHANN WOLFGANG VON GOETHE

(Goethe lived in Germany around two hundred years ago and was a writer, poet, scientist, and philosopher — brainy people back then put their fingers in a lot of pies. It seems to me to be just the sort of thinking we need now: dream it, do it, do it now.)

Seeing the Future

How would you like to bike to college or to work on tree-covered paths and live in a house where the roof tiles made the electricity for the lights and collected water to run the tap? How would you like to work in an office with flood defenses on the ground floor and a wind turbine on the roof? How would you like to live without traffic jams, and travel in high-speed trains? How would you like your town to be such a clean, green, unpolluted place to live that you never thought of going on foreign vacation?

This is the future that Professor Mark Maslin, leading climate scientist at University College London, thinks is possible for humanity:

"This is what the world would look like in fifty years if we shifted to a low-carbon economy."

It sounds wonderful, but how are we going to get to Mark's rosy future? He thinks the best and most effective way is by making the world a FAIRER place.

"There are two major problems facing humanity in the twenty-first century: global poverty and global warming," says Mark. And he thinks we can tackle them both together.

Poor countries want to improve the lives of their people, to make sure that everyone gets enough to eat, a place to live, education, and health care. All that takes energy. If the energy comes from cheap fossil fuels, then however much emissions-cutting the rich countries do, it won't make any difference.

"China is building a new coal-fired power station every four days," says Mark. **"That's going to make global warming worse."**

Mark Maslin

Mark Maslin in the Arctic in 2007, when he took twelve teenagers along to educate them in the science and art of climate change

The alternative is to pay developing countries to use energy sources and other technologies with low emissions. This would work through what's called a "cap and trade" system. This means that rich countries would set a limit on the volume of greenhouse gases they were allowed to emit—a "cap." To reach that target they'd have to cut emissions, increase energy efficiency, and start to use renewables as a source of energy. But they could also "trade," which means they'd pay a poor country to start using new low-emission technology—and the amount of emissions this would save could add to the rich country's tally of emissions cuts. The "caps" would be set at lower and lower levels, to reduce the rich countries' emissions bit by bit and keep a steady flow of money and clean technology going to poorer countries.

A system like this has been used in the U.S. to make industries cut their emissions of other polluting gases, such as sulfur dioxide. What's more, it was much, much cheaper to do than anyone expected.

"Cap and trade" could mean that everyone wins, Mark says, because:

"Poor countries get richer, and rich countries get cleaner!"

As a scientist, Mark sees the solutions very clearly, but he knows that to change things, science must engage with politics and business. He talks to politicians and businesspeople and puts them in touch with other top climate scientists.

"My tightrope walk is between giving people good, reliable scientific information and not telling them how to do their job."

There are U.N. climate-change talks happening as I write this in May

2010, and they will go on happening every year until the world has come up with a real plan of action for fighting climate change. Mark would like to see a "cap and trade" system that involved the U.S. (the biggest greenhouse-gas emitter now) and India and China (who will be the biggest greenhouse-gas emitters in thirty years' time). Mark would also like to see an agreement to "contract and converge"—which means people in rich countries "contracting" their carbon footprint so that they are nearer to (they "converge" with) the carbon footprint of people in poor countries, so we'd end up with a small carbon footprint for everyone in the world. Mark says:

"In my opinion, global warming is good for humanity: for the first time in humanity's history, we have to tackle the unequal distribution of global wealth."

Mark's hopefulness about our future comes from his studies of our past—of human evolution over the last 100,000 years:

"We're the greatest weed the planet has ever produced. We can survive anything!" he jokes.

But of course it would be nice if humans did a bit more than just "survive" and end up chewing on bones around a campfire of old sofas. It would be nice to hold on to civilization, and to do that we must have something to aim for:

"If we can have a vision of the future that's worth working for, then we can get there. All the solutions exist, and there's no barrier to achieving a very different world from the one we live in now."

FUTURE CITY

A few years ago, China developed a plan to build an "eco-city" called Dongtan. All its energy would come from renewables, and its food would be grown nearby to reduce food miles. Though the plan has fallen behind schedule, it still gives us an idea of what such a city could look like.

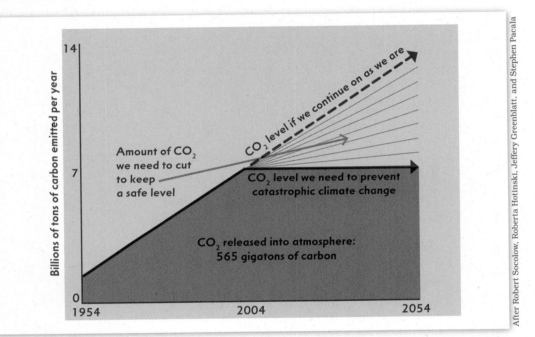

Billions of tons of carbon emitted per year

Amount of CO_2 we need to cut to keep a safe level

CO_2 level if we continue on as we are

CO_2 level we need to prevent catastrophic climate change

CO_2 released into atmosphere: 565 gigatons of carbon

After Robert Socolow, Roberta Hotinski, Jeffery Greenblatt, and Stephen Pacala

GET A WEDGIE FOR GAIA!

In spite of the slow progress with international agreements on cutting emissions, many people are waking up to the fact that cuts have got to be DRASTIC. This can seem pretty daunting, but U.S. scientists Stephen Pacala and Robert Socolow of Princeton University have come up with a brilliant idea called wedge theory, which has climate experts, campaigners, and politicians very excited.

Just imagine the graph of greenhouse gases in the atmosphere, rising up over time like a steep hill. Now imagine that graph flattening out, with no more rises after this moment. What you're left with is a fat wedge between where we want emissions to be — not rising — and where they are going right now — up and up. This wedge shows the greenhouse gas we have got to STOP emitting — roughly 7 billion tons per year by 2054. Stephen and Robert's idea was to break that mega wedge down into seven smaller wedges, and then find ways to get rid of them. It was easy!

There are fifteen different ways to get rid of those seven wedges, right now, using what we already know, including the following:

> ❱ Using low-energy lightbulbs and other efficient electrical gear in homes and businesses takes care of one whole wedge. One down, six to go . . . .
> ❱ Doubling the fuel economy of cars (how many miles they get to the gallon), and halving the distance we travel by car, takes care of two wedges.
> ❱ Stopping deforestation and doubling our rate of tree-planting — another wedge.

Just doing three simple things takes care of half the cuts we need . . . and there are twelve more options on the list for making wedges disappear.

You can even play this as a game. Check out the website:

cmi.princeton.edu/wedges

"It always seems impossible until it's done."

NELSON MANDELA

(Mandela was the first democratically elected president of South Africa. He spent twenty-seven years in prison because he stuck up for freedom and equality for all South Africa's people. So he knows a lot about achieving impossible things.)

CONCLUSION

When I started writing this book, I was pretty gloomy. Climate change **was** big and scary, and I **didn't** think I, or anyone else, could make a difference. But I'm not gloomy anymore. In fact, I'm quite excited, because I've started to hear a sound, sometimes like a distant rumble of thunder, sometimes like a raindrop close to my ear. It's the sound of people changing. It's there in all the conversations I had with the people in this book; it's there in all the practical details about insulating houses or designing electric cars; it's there even in all the wrangling of U.N. climate negotiations. I think there's a shift happening in people's hearts and minds, not just toward the need to save our skins from climate change, but toward a more deeply respectful relationship with the planet that's given us life. It could be the sound of our species finally growing up.

Sandy Lovelock

Section Three

Afterword

by James Lovelock

"Gaia warriors" is a wonderfully surprising phrase, but it is the right title for this book. Some people see Gaia as the mother of everything alive, all-powerful, with a religious significance as part of God's creation; others as the name of a scientific theory about the Earth system. I see her as something that includes both of these ideas, and if we accept, despite pretending otherwise, that humans are war-loving animals, the words "Gaia" and "warriors" do indeed go together.

Warriors do not march to have a friendly discussion, or even an argument. Warriors march to battle, and they usually intend to win and make sure that their beliefs prevail. Almost all human history is made up of brief spells of peace interspersed with long periods of war, and whenever war happened and whatever side we were on, we convinced ourselves that we were in the right and that the war was just.

In this, the twenty-first century, warriors may be faced with an older and simpler form of conflict: that of fighting for survival.

Unconsciously we set in motion the conditions for this war two centuries ago when we began to take more from the earth than we could ever pay back.

It was not simply by using fossil fuels for energy but also by taking the natural forests and turning them into farmland. These two acts, which made food and medicine abundant, enabled our numbers to grow until we took more from Gaia than she could give. Now we are like the victim of a loan shark, with debts larger than our means to repay them.

Gaia, the Earth system, regulates the planet so it always remains habitable, but to do so she needs the natural forest ecosystems intact. What we humans have done by taking them for ourselves alone is to make the earth uninhabitable. I think it unlikely that anything we do will alter the course of this change. Nobody—not the cleverest scientist nor even a committee made up of Nobel Prize winners from each of the sciences—can with certainty predict the world of 2030 and tell us how to live peacefully there. Nor can they tell us how to restore the earth to the lush and habitable state it was in sixty years ago. There are no sure answers, and Gaia, the Earth system, is moving faster than we can respond, let alone oppose its motion.

Survival is our only option, and before long, some people will find that their part of the earth is less harmed by climate change than others. Naturally those whose land becomes desert or is flooded and can no longer provide food and water will move to where there is plenty. Because of our natures, war between these haves and have-nots is inevitable. There will not be food and water enough for both. Sometimes the invaders will win, and other times the defenders; what matters is that there are survivors so that there continue to be humans on the earth. The ultimate survivors will probably include some powerfully effective Gaia warriors, and we will have evolved another step toward a new and perhaps more intelligent species of humans.

What a wicked, wasteful way of progressing, you may think. But war is like this, and never forget that evolution by natural selection is also a blind, cruel process. How else could a feathered monstrosity of the Jurassic evolve into the exquisite perfection of a streamlined swallow? The answer is that countless numbers of less-perfect losers lost in that passage to perfection.

> ❝ **Nobody . . . can with certainty predict the world of 2030 and tell us how to live peacefully there.** ❞

To turn the clumsy animals that we are now into streamlined intelligences that can serve as the information system and warriors of our planet will not happen quickly or easily.

Other organisms, more important than we are, started as disastrous mistakes whose unrestrained growth did massive planetwide damage. Tiny green bacteria heedlessly polluted the air more than 2 billion years ago with a poisonous, destructive gas: oxygen—pollution far more deadly than anything we have done so far. Yet evolution allowed Gaia to adapt and then use oxygen to support life. It took more than a billion years, but from those first polluting bacteria there evolved all planetary life, even giant redwood trees and a world that animals could inhabit.

It has taken Gaia 3.5 billion years, more than a quarter the age of the universe, to evolve humans, a social animal intelligent enough and capable enough to show her how stunningly beautiful she is when seen from space through the eyes of astronauts and when compared with her dead siblings, Mars and Venus. We are a part of Gaia, as are all things alive, whether tigers or slime molds, and consequently our thoughts are hers. Through us, she begins to understand her history and place in the universe.

Let us look forward to the time when our descendants have evolved to become Gaia's brain—clear in thought and clear in vision—and Gaia's T cells, her warriors, the true defenders serving the first intelligent planet in our galaxy.

MORE GOOD PLACES TO GET INFORMATION

WEBSITES

The Hadley Centre for Climate Change Research
Really good, clear information on the science of climate change:
www.metoffice.gov.uk/research/hadleycentre/

NASA Climate Change Page
climate.nasa.gov

National Oceanic and Atmospheric Administration, Global Warming Page
www.ncdc.noaa.gov/oa/climate/globalwarming.html

National Geographic, Climate Change Page
environment.nationalgeographic.com/environmental/global-warming/

BOOKS

Global Warming: A Very Short Introduction by Mark Maslin
Takes you through all the science, politics, and potential solutions to a very positive vision of human future.

The Rough Guide to Climate Change by Robert Henson
Well explained, really clear, and nicely written.

(If you read just one book, it should be one of the two above.)

Heat by George Monbiot
Good ways of getting out of the mess we're in.

The Revenge of Gaia by James Lovelock
Really beautifully written explanation of what Gaia is, how she controls our climate, and the science of how we've messed it all up.

Funny Weather: Everything You Didn't Want to Know About Climate Change But Probably Should Find Out by Kate Evans
Funny, clear, and easy-to-read cartoon guide to the basics.

GLOSSARY

Greenhouse gas is any gas in the atmosphere that traps heat and prevents it from escaping to space. The gases that make up most of the atmosphere—nitrogen and oxygen—don't do this, but some of the gases that are found at quite low concentrations do have this heat-trapping effect.

Main greenhouse gases
CO_2 (carbon dioxide): a natural part of the atmosphere, taken up by living plants and breathed out by animals and plants and released from their bodies as they die and decay. Also released when anything burns, so that human burning of fossil fuels—coal, gas, and oil—greatly increases the amount of carbon dioxide in the atmosphere, where it stays for a hundred years.

CH_4 (methane): has a much more powerful heat-trapping effect than carbon dioxide, but luckily there's much less of it around and it survives just ten years in the atmosphere. Released from wetlands, rice fields, and domestic animals, and could be released from natural stores deep under the oceans if the seas warm too much.

Water vapor: a natural part of the atmosphere, without which clouds couldn't form and rain wouldn't fall. A weak heat-trapper, but still has a big heating effect because there is so much of it—and more and more as the earth gets warmer.

Ozone: a natural part of the atmosphere, protecting us from harmful parts of the sun's rays. It's also released when sunlight shines on certain pollutants. In the wrong place and in the wrong quantities, it can interfere with heat loss from the upper atmosphere.

Other greenhouse gases that exist in very small amounts include CFCs (chlorofluorocarbons) and nitrous oxide, both released from industrial processes.

Paleoclimatology is the study of climate in the distant past. Paleoclimatologists look at sediments from ancient lakes, ice cores, tree rings, coral reefs, and even ancient tribal records, working like detectives to track down evidence of what Earth's climate and atmosphere were like in the past. Understanding how climate changed in the past helps to predict how man-made climate change will affect the planet in the future.

IPCC (Intergovernmental Panel on Climate Change) is a big cooperative project involving hundreds of top scientists from countries all over the world. They work together to study all the very best research on climate and climate change. They put it all together in very detailed reports that help governments decide what should be done about climate change. These excellent reports are available to anyone on the Internet.

Carbon footprint is a measure of the quantity of greenhouse-gas emissions a person, an organization, or even a whole country is giving off. It is calculated by adding up the direct emissions—say, from your central heating boiler or the car you drive—and the indirect ones, like the emissions that were created by growing the food you eat or by making the products and services you use. It can be a very tricky calculation for big organizations or countries, and even for individuals, but it can help to show what are the best changes to make to reduce emissions most.

Carbon offsetting is the idea that you can cancel out some of your carbon footprint by paying for something to happen that soaks up greenhouse gases—such as planting a tree, saving a bit of rain forest, or installing low-energy light-bulbs or solar power. It's a good idea, but sometimes the companies that offer offsetting are just in it for money and have very little REAL impact on emissions. So choose carefully—or, better still, CUT the size of your footprint AND pay for something that takes some greenhouse gases out of the atmosphere.

Carbon trading is really just offsetting on a big scale—that of huge companies or even whole countries. The basic idea is that rich countries that produce the most greenhouse gases pay poor countries to keep their footprint small and introduce low-carbon technology instead of the old-fashioned energy-guzzling sort. At its best, it could mean that poor countries get their hands on some of the rich countries' money and get free new clean-and-green technology. At its worst, it could mean keeping poor countries back and allowing rich countries to go on belching out greenhouse gases as always.

Cap and trade could be a way of making carbon trading work at its best. The idea is that a limit, or cap, is set on the amount of greenhouse gases any country can emit. This limit is lowered year by year so that the total amount of greenhouse gases spewed out goes down. To keep within their limit, countries can either just cut their emissions or both cut and trade emissions with other countries whose carbon footprint is so low they don't even have to cut to meet their limit. But the limits still fall year by year, so all countries end up with a similar, smaller footprint.

Gulf Stream is the commonly used name for part of the Atlantic thermohaline circulation, which is the warm, salty current of water that flows up from the South Atlantic, past the west coast of Britain, and up to the Arctic, where it cools, sinks, and flows south again. It's just part of the giant system of currents that carry the warmth of the tropics and the cool of the poles around the globe, helping to create familiar patterns of climate. One of the possible outcomes of climate change is the disruption of these currents, such as the shutting down of the Gulf Stream, which helps to keep Britain mild and wet.

INDEX

ACKNOWLEDGMENTS

With thanks to Beth Aves, Genevieve Herr, Neil Jennings, Sylvia Knight, Sandy Lovelock, Mark Maslin, and Caz Royds.

Also to the organizations that helped, including U.K. Youth Climate Coalition, Footprint Friends, CarbonSense, World Land Trust, Royal Meteorological Society, and Tipping Point.

The author and publishers wish to thank all those who so generously gave of their time and supplied photographs and diagrams for this book.

Every effort has been made to secure permission for the use of copyright material. If notified of any error or omission, the publisher will gladly make the necessary correction in future printings.

Website addresses/links were correct at the time of printing.